A New Structural Transformation of the Public Sphere and Deliberative Politics

T0019697

Jürgen Habermas

A New Structural Transformation of the Public Sphere and Deliberative Politics

Translated by Ciaran Cronin

polity

Originally published in German as *Ein neuer Strukturwandel der Öffentlichkeit und die deliberative Politik* © Suhrkamp Verlag AG Berlin 2022. All rights reserved by and controlled through Suhrkamp Verlag Berlin.

This English edition © Polity Press, 2023

Polity Press
65 Bridge Street
Cambridge CB2 1UR, UK

Polity Press
111 River Street
Hoboken, NJ 07030, USA

All rights reserved. Except for the quotation of short passages for the purpose of criticism and review, no part of this publication may be reproduced, stored in a retrieval system or transmitted, in any form or by any means, electronic, mechanical, photocopying, recording or otherwise, without the prior permission of the publisher.

ISBN-13: 978-1-5095-5893-3
ISBN-13: 978-1-5095-5894-0 (pb)

A catalogue record for this book is available from the British Library.

Library of Congress Control Number: 2023934596

Typeset in 10.25 on 15 pt Plantin MT
by Fakenham Prepress Solutions, Fakenham, Norfolk NR21 8NL
Printed and bound in Great Britain by TJ Books Ltd, Padstow, Cornwall

The publisher has used its best endeavours to ensure that the URLs for external websites referred to in this book are correct and active at the time of going to press. However, the publisher has no responsibility for the websites and can make no guarantee that a site will remain live or that the content is or will remain appropriate.

Every effort has been made to trace all copyright holders, but if any have been overlooked the publisher will be pleased to include any necessary credits in any subsequent reprint or edition.

For further information on Polity, visit our website:
politybooks.com

Contents

Preface

I would like to thank my colleagues Martin Seeliger and Sebastian Sevignani, whose current work on whether we must speak of a 'new' structural transformation of the public sphere has prompted me to revisit an old topic, even though I have long since turned my attention to different questions and only take very selective note of the relevant publications. In return, the contributions they have collected in a special issue of the journal *Leviathan*, which has appeared in the meantime, have enabled me to get up to speed on the current state of the professional discussion.[1] I would like thank all of the contributors for the instructive reading.

Not altogether surprisingly, the topic is attracting widespread interest today. Therefore, I have decided to make a slightly revised version of my own contribution to the aforementioned collection available to a more general audience. This essay is supplemented with two clarificatory texts on the concept of deliberative politics, which depends on enlightened democratic will formation in the political public sphere. These texts consist of an abridged version of an interview conducted for the *Oxford Handbook on Deliberative Democracy*[2] and an adaptation of my foreword to a volume of interviews on the same topic edited by Emilie Prattico.[3]

Jürgen Habermas
Starnberg, January 2022

Reflections and Conjectures on a New Structural Transformation of the Public Sphere[1]

As the author of the book *Structural Transformation of the Public Sphere*, originally published in German nearly six decades ago and chosen by Martin Seeliger and Sebastian Sevignani as the starting point for their edited collection of papers,[2] I would like to make two remarks. Judging by sales, the book, although it was my first, has remained my most successful to date. The second remark concerns the reason that I suspect accounts for this unusual reception: the book contains a social and conceptual history of the 'public sphere' that attracted a great deal of criticism but also provided new stimuli for more wide-ranging historical research. This historical aspect is not my topic here. But for the social sciences, it had the effect of embedding the political concept of the 'public sphere' in a wider socio-structural context. Until then, the term had been used in a rather unspecific sense, primarily within the conceptual field of 'public opinion' understood since Lazarsfeld in demoscopic terms; by contrast, my study conceptualized the public sphere in sociological terms and assigned it a place within the functionally differentiated structure of modern societies between civil society and the political system. This meant that it could also be studied with a view to its functional contribution to social integration and, in particular, to the political integration of the citizens.[3] I am aware that the social significance of the public sphere extends far beyond its contribution to democratic will formation in constitutional states;[4] nevertheless, I also discussed it subsequently from the perspective of political theory.[5] In the present text, too, I take as my starting point the function of the public sphere in ensuring the continued existence of the democratic political community.

I will begin by addressing the relationship between normative and empirical theory (1), before going on to explain why and how we should understand the democratic process, once it is institutionalized under social conditions marked by individualism and pluralism, in the light of deliberative politics (2), and concluding these preliminary theoretical reflections by recalling the improbable conditions that must be fulfilled if a crisis-prone capitalist democracy is to remain stable (3). Within this theoretical framework, for which *Structural*

Transformation provided a preliminary social-historical analysis, I will outline how digitalization is transforming the structure of the media and the impact that this transformation is having on the political process. The technological advance marked by digitalized communication initially fosters trends towards the dissolution of boundaries, but also towards the fragmentation of the public sphere. The platform character of the new media is creating, alongside the editorial public sphere, a space of communication in which readers, listeners and viewers can spontaneously assume the role of authors (4). The reach of the new media is shown by the findings of a longitudinal survey on the usage of the expanded media offerings in Germany. While internet usage has increased rapidly over the past two decades and both television and radio have been largely able to hold their ground, consumption of printed newspapers and magazines has plummeted (5). The rise of the new media is taking place in the shadow of the commercial exploitation of the currently virtually unregulated internet communication. On the one hand, this is threatening to undermine the economic basis of the traditional newspaper publishers and of journalists as the responsible occupational group; on the other hand, a mode of semi-public, fragmented and self-enclosed communication seems to be spreading among exclusive users of social media that is distorting their *perception of the political public sphere* as such. If this conjecture is correct, an important subjective prerequisite for a more or less deliberative mode of opinion and will formation is jeopardized among an increasing portion of the citizenry (6).

(1) In studies dealing with the role of the political public sphere in constitutional democracies, we generally distinguish between empirical investigations and normative theories – John Rawls speaks in this connection of 'ideal theory'. This alternative involves an oversimplification. In my view, the role of democratic theory is to reconstruct the rational content of the norms and practices that have acquired positive validity since the constitutional revolutions of the late eighteenth century and, as such, have become part of historical reality. The very fact that empirical studies of processes of opinion formation under democratic conditions become pointless if these studies are not *also* interpreted in the light of the normative *requirements* these processes are supposed to satisfy in constitutional democracies, highlights an interesting circumstance. However, understanding this calls for a brief historical digression. For the revolutionary acts that endowed basic rights with positive validity first made citizens aware of a new *normative gradient* [*normatives Gefälle*] that as a result became part of *social reality* itself.

4

The peculiarly demanding normativity of constitutional orders founded on basic rights is a function of their 'unsaturated' character, in virtue of which they point beyond the status quo. This historical fact can be better understood against the backdrop of the customary form of social normativity. Social phenomena, be they actions, flows of communication or artefacts, values or norms, habits or institutions, contracts or organizations, have a rule-governed character. This is shown by the possibility of deviant behaviour: rules can be followed or broken. Different kinds of rules exist: logical, mathematical and grammatical rules, game rules and instrumental and social rules of action, which can be differentiated according to strategic and normatively regulated interactions. It is the latter norms, in particular, that are distinguished by the peculiar mode of validity of the 'ought'.[6] As the nature of the sanctions for deviant behaviour shows, such normative behavioural expectations may make *more or less strict* demands, with morality imposing the most stringent demands. The distinguishing feature of the *universalistic moral conceptions* that arose with the worldviews of the axial age is that they call for the equal treatment of all persons in principle. In the course of the European Enlightenment, this moral-cognitive potential became detached from the respective religious or metaphysical background and was differentiated in such a way that – according to the still authoritative Kantian tenor – each person, in his or her inalienable individuality, *ought to* be accorded equal respect and receive equal treatment. On this conception, each person's conduct must be judged, taking his or her individual situation into consideration, in accordance with precisely those general norms that are equally good for everyone from the discursively examined standpoint of all those possibly affected.

A particular sociological implication of this development is especially interesting in the present context. We must recall the singularly radical character of rational morality if we want to gauge the steep normative gradient of the oughtness claim [*Fallhöhe des Sollensanspruchs*] raised by this egalitarian-individualistic universalism. Moreover, switching perspective from rational *morality* to the rational *law* inspired by this morality, this radicalness is also essential for understanding the historical significance of the fact that, since the first two constitutional revolutions, this exacting moral-cognitive potential has formed the core of the basic rights sanctioned by the state, and thus of positive law in general. With the 'declaration' of the basic rights and human rights, the substance of rational morality migrated into the medium of binding constitutional law constructed out of subjective rights! With those *historically unprecedented* founding acts that give rise to democratic constitutional orders in the late eighteenth century, the *hitherto unknown* tension of a normative gradient lodged itself in the political consciousness of legally free and equal citizens. This encouragement to develop a new normative self-understanding went hand in hand with a new historical consciousness turned offensively towards the future, as Reinhard Koselleck has demonstrated. Taken as a whole, it amounted to a complex shift in consciousness embedded in the capitalist dynamics of a transformation of conditions of social life that is simultaneously accelerated by technological progress. In the meantime, however, this dynamic has provoked a more defensive mindset in Western societies, one which feels overwhelmed rather than energized by the technologically and economically propelled growth in societal complexity. But the enduring social movements that repeatedly reawaken the consciousness of the incomplete inclusion of oppressed, marginalized, degraded, afflicted, exploited and disadvantaged groups, classes, subcultures, genders, races, nations and continents, are a reminder of the gap between the positive validity and the still *unsaturated content* of the human rights that, in the meantime, have been 'declared' not only at the national level.[7] Hence – and this is the point of my digression – among the preconditions of the survival of a democratic polity is that the citizens should see themselves from the participant perspective as being involved in the process of progressively realizing the basic rights, which, although they have not been *exhausted*, already enjoy positive *validity*.

Quite apart from these long-term processes through which the basic rights are realized, what interests me is the *normal case* in which the status of free and equal citizens in a democratically constituted polity is associated with certain taken-for-granted *idealizations*. For when the citizens *participate* in their civic practices, they cannot avoid making the intuitive (and counter-factual) *assumption* that the civil rights they practise generally deliver on what they promise. Especially with a view to the stability of the political system, the normative core of the democratic constitution must be anchored in civic consciousness, that is, in the citizens' own implicit beliefs. It is not the philosophers, but the large majority of the citizens, who must be intuitively convinced of the constitutional principles. On the other hand, they must also have *confidence* that their votes count equally in democratic elections, that legislation and jurisdiction, the actions of government and the administration, are mostly above board, and that, as a general rule, there is a fair opportunity to revise dubious decisions. Even though these expectations are *idealizations* that the actual practice sometimes falls short of to a greater or lesser extent, they create social facts insofar as they are reflected in the citizens' judgements and conduct. What is problematic about such practices is not the idealizing assumptions they demand of their participants, but the credibility of the institutions, which must not openly and enduringly repudiate these idealizations. Trump's fatal exhortation would hardly have met with the intended furious response of the citizens who stormed the Capitol on 6 January 2021 if the political elites had not for decades disappointed the legitimate, constitutionally guaranteed expectations of a significant portion of their citizens. Hence, the design of a political theory tailored to this kind of constitutional state must be such that it does justice both to the peculiar *idealizing surplus* of a morally based system of basic rights – a surplus that imbues the citizens with a consciousness of being involved in the exercise of democratically legitimized government – as well as to the social and institutional conditions which lend *credibility* to the idealizations that the citizens necessarily associate with their practices.

A theory of democracy, therefore, does not need to undertake the task of designing, i.e. *constructing* and justifying, the principles of a just political order on its own in order to instil them in the citizens like a teacher; in other words, it does not have to understand itself as a normatively *designed* theory. Its task is instead to *rationally reconstruct* such principles from existing law and from the corresponding intuitive expectations and conceptions of legitimacy of the citizens. It must render the fundamental meaning of the historically *established* and *proven*, and hence sufficiently stable, constitutional orders explicit and explain the justifying reasons that can invest the de facto exercise of government with actual legitimizing power in the eyes of their citizens, and therefore also ensure civic participation.[8] That political theory, by making *explicit* the implicit consciousness of the mass of the citizens who participate in political life, can in turn *shape* their normative self-understanding is no more unusual than the role of academic history of the present, which performatively influences the further course of the historical events it describes. This does not mean that political theory plays an inherently pedagogical role vis-à-vis politics. Therefore, I do not see deliberative politics as a far-fetched ideal against which sordid reality must be measured, but as an existential precondition in pluralistic societies of any democracy worthy of the name.[9] The more heterogeneous a society's conditions of life, cultural forms of life and individual lifestyles are, the more the lack of an a fortiori *existing* background consensus must be counterbalanced by the commonality of public opinion and will *formation*.

Because the origins of the classical theories predate the constitutional revolutions of the late eighteenth century, they could present themselves as normative blueprints for establishing democratic constitutions.

However, a contemporary political theory can simply take note of the fact that the exacting democratic constitutional idea introduces a *tension* between the positive *validity* of binding constitutional norms and the constitutional *reality* into *the very reality* of modern societies and that, when extreme dissonances become apparent, this tension can still trigger the mobilizing dynamic of mass protests. Hence, such a theory must recognize that its task is *re*constructive in nature. Both the republican and the liberal theoretical traditions, however, already distort this idea by *one-sidedly* according priority either to *popular sovereignty* or to the *rule of law*, and thereby miss the point that individually exercised subjective freedoms and intersubjectively exercised popular sovereignty are equally original. For the idea underlying those two constitutional revolutions is the foundation of a *self-determined* association of *free consociates under law*: the latter, as democratic co-legislators, must ultimately grant themselves their freedom through the *equal distribution of subjective rights in accordance with general laws*. According to this idea of collective self-determination, which combines the egalitarian universalism of equal rights for all with the individualism of each subject, *democracy* and the *rule of law* are on a par. And only a discourse theory that revolves around the idea of deliberative politics can do justice to this idea.[10]

(2) The approach of deliberative politics can be traced back to the early liberal world of ideas of the *Vormärz* period.[11] In the meantime, however, it has unfolded in the context of the welfare state, its chief merit being that it explains how, in pluralistic societies that lack a shared religion or worldview, political compromises can be reached against the background of an intuitive constitutional consensus. The secularization of state power gave rise to a gap in legitimation. Because the belief that the ruling dynasties were divinely ordained no longer sufficed to legitimize them in modern societies, the democratic system had to legitimize itself *out of its own resources*, as it were, through the legitimacy-*generating* power of the legally institutionalized *procedure* of democratic will formation. Religious conceptions of legitimacy were not replaced by a different idea, but instead by the *procedure* of democratic self-empowerment, which is institutionalized in the form of equally distributed subjective rights, so that it can be exercised by free and equal citizens. At first glance, it seems quite mysterious how the legal institutionalization of a procedure of democratic *will* formation – in other words, sheer 'legality' – could nevertheless give rise to the 'legitimacy' of universally *convincing* results. Essential to explaining this is the analysis of the meaning that this procedure acquires from the perspective of the participants. It

owes its persuasiveness to an improbable combination of two conditions: on the one hand, the procedure calls for the *inclusion of all those affected* by possible decisions as equal participants in the political decision-making process; on the other hand, it makes the democratic decisions in which all individuals are involved together dependent on the more or less pronounced *discursive character* of the preceding *deliberations*. As a result, the inclusive formation of *will* becomes contingent on the *force of the reasons* mobilized during the preceding process of *opinion* formation. *Inclusion* corresponds to the democratic requirement that all those affected should have equal rights to participate in political will formation, while the filter of *deliberation* takes into account the expectation that solutions to problems should be cognitively correct and viable, and *grounds* the *assumption* that the results are rationally acceptable. This assumption can be justified, in turn, by the falsifiable *supposition* that, in the consultations leading up to a majority decision, all relevant topics, requisite information and suitable proposals for solutions are discussed as far as possible with arguments pro and contra. And it is this *requirement of free deliberation* that explains the central *role of the political public sphere*.[12] Incidentally, this abstract consideration is confirmed by the historical fact that something like a 'bourgeois public sphere' emerged at the same time as liberal democracy, first in England and then in the United States, France and other European countries.

However, those two requirements of the democratic process – namely, deliberation and the inclusion of all citizens – can be realized even approximately only at the level of the institutions of the state, and above all in the representative bodies of parliamentary lawmaking. This explains the *essential* but *limited* contribution that *political communication in the public sphere* can make to the democratic process. Its contribution is *essential* because it represents the sole locus where public opinion and political will are formed in a manner that in principle includes *in corpore* all adult citizens who are eligible to vote. And this can, in turn, motivate the decisions that citizens make together, but as individuals and in the isolation of the voting booth – that is, 'of their own free will'. These electoral decisions lead to an outcome binding on all citizens insofar as they determine the party political composition of parliament and, directly or indirectly, of the government. At the same time, the contribution of the political public sphere to democratic opinion and will formation is *limited* because, as a general rule, no collectively binding individual decisions are taken there (only in rare cases do fundamental questions have such a clear structure that they can be decided by such plebiscites). The formation of opinion steered by the mass media gives rise to a plurality of *public opinions* among the dispersed public of citizens. These public opinions, which are compiled out of topics, contributions and information, and thus acquire a distinctive profile, compete over the relevant issues, the correct policy goals and the best problem-solving strategies.

One circumstance is especially relevant in our context: the overall influence that the will of the citizens, hence of the sovereign, acquires over the decisions of the political system depends essentially on the *enlightening quality* of the contribution of the mass media to this formation of opinion. This is because opinion formation is sustained by the prior processing by the professional media of the topics and contributions, alternative proposals, information and supporting and opposing positions – in short, of the input fed into the public sphere via the information channels of, among others, the political parties, the interest groups and PR agencies, and the societal subsystems, as well as by civil society organizations and intellectuals. This more or less *informed pluralism of opinion* filtered by the media system gives every citizen the opportunity to form his or her *own* opinion and to make *an election decision* that is *rationally motivated* from his or her point of view. However, the competition of opinions and decisions within the public sphere itself remains open; here deliberation is still separate from the decisions of the individual voters, because the elections to parliament are only prepared in the public sphere. It is only beyond the threshold of general elections that the elected members of parliament can consult and decide *with each other* in accordance with democratic procedures. Only in the representative bodies and the other state institutions, and in an especially formal way in the courts, are procedural rules tailored to the deliberative format of opinion and will formation that justifies the presumption that majority decisions are more or less rationally acceptable.

In order to correctly assess the *limited contribution* that the political public sphere can make, we must examine the organizational section of the constitutional text and the structural division of labour within the political system *as a whole* and read it like a flow chart. It then becomes apparent how the democratic current of the citizens' opinion and will formation branches out beyond the threshold of elections and is directed into the channels – besieged by the lobbying of the functional systems – of party politics, legislation, jurisdiction, administration and government. It ultimately flows into the decisions stemming – within the framework of the law – from compromises between functional imperatives, political and social interests and voter preferences. The legitimate political results are then evaluated and criticized in turn in the political public sphere and are processed into new voter preferences after the conclusion of legislative terms. The assumption that political discourses are also *oriented* to the *goal* of reaching an agreement is often misunderstood. It by no means implies an idealistic conception of the democratic process as something like a convivial university seminar. On the contrary, one can assume that the orientation of reasonable participants to the truth or correctness of their argued convictions adds even more fuel to the fire of political disputes and lends them a fundamentally *agonal character.* To argue is to contradict. It is only the right – and, indeed, the encouragement – to say 'no' to each other that elicits the epistemic potential of conflicting opinions in discourse; for the latter is geared to the self-correction of participants who, without mutual criticism, could not *learn from one another.* The point of deliberative politics is, after all, that it enables us to *improve* our beliefs in political disputes and get *closer* to correct solutions to problems. In the cacophony of conflicting opinions unleashed in the public sphere only one thing is presupposed – the consensus on the shared constitutional principles that legitimizes all other disputes. Against this consensual backdrop, the whole democratic process consists of a tide of dissent that is stirred up over and over again by the citizens' search for rationally acceptable decisions oriented to the truth.

The deliberative character of the opinion and will formation of the voters is measured *in the political public sphere* by the discursive quality of the contributions, not by the goal of a consensus, which is in any case unattainable; rather, here the participants' orientation to the truth is supposed to ignite an open-ended conflict of opinions that gives rise to *competing* public opinions. This dynamic of *enduring* dissent in the public sphere likewise shapes the competition between parties and the antagonism between government and opposition, as well as differences of opinion among experts. The arguments mobilized in this way can then inform the binding decisions to be taken in a procedurally correct manner in the corresponding fora of the political system. All that is required to institutionalize the anarchic power of saying 'no' unleashed in public debates and election campaigns, in disputes between political parties, in the negotiations of parliament and its committees, and in the deliberations of the government and the courts, is the *prior political integration* of all participants into the consensus over the basic intention of their constitution. The latter is simple enough: it merely spells out the plain will of the citizens to *obey only the laws they have given themselves*. Without such a consensus on the *meaning* of deliberative democratic self-legislation, the respective minorities would not have any reason to submit to majoritarian decisions, for the time being at least. In making this point, however, we must not lose sight of the main factor on which the fate of a democracy depends: judged from this normative standpoint, the institutionalized formation of political will must also actually function on the whole in such a way that the voters' constitutional consensus is *confirmed by experience* from time to time. In other words, there must be a *recognizable* connection between the results of government action and the input of the voters' decisions, such that the citizens can recognize it as the confirmation of the rationalizing power of their own democratic opinion and will formation.[13] The citizens must be able to *perceive* their conflict of opinions as both consequential and as a dispute over the better reasons.[14]

'But this is at odds with reality', one might object, even now in the oldest Anglo-Saxon democracies. The approval that the storming of the Capitol met with among Trump voters must probably also be understood as the emotive response of voters who for decades have lacked a sense that their neglected interests are taken seriously by the political system in concrete, discernible ways. The dynamic of political regression into which almost all Western democracies have been drawn since the turn of the millennium can be measured by the decline, and in some countries virtually the demise, of this *rationalizing power* of public debates. This dependence of the

problem-solving power of a democracy on the flow of deliberative politics highlights the central role of the political
public sphere.

Without a suitable context, however, the essential
preconditions of deliberative politics for the democratic
legitimization of government cannot gain traction
among a population from which, after all, 'all authority'
is supposed to be 'derived'.[15] Government action,
landmark decisions of the higher courts, parliamentary
legislation, competition between political parties and
free political elections call for an active citizenry, because
the political public sphere is rooted in a civil society
which – as the sounding board for the disruptions of
major functional systems in need of repair – establishes
the communicative connections between politics and
its social 'environments'. However, civil society can
only serve as a kind of early-warning system for policy-
makers if it brings forth the actors who organize public
attention for the relevant issues that are preoccupying
citizens. In the large territorial societies of the modern
Western democracies, however, there has always been a
tension between the functionally required level of civic
commitment and the private and personal obligations
and interests that *public citizens* [*Staatsbürger*] both
want to and need to fulfil in their role as *private citizens*
[*Gesellschaftsbürger*]. This structural conflict between the
public and private roles of citizens is also reflected in

the public sphere itself. In Europe, the bourgeois public sphere in its literary and its political form was only gradually able to free itself from the shadow of older formations – above all the religious public sphere of ecclesiastical government and the representative public sphere of the personal rule embodied in emperors, kings and princes – once the social-structural prerequisites for a *functional separation of state and society*, of the public from the private economic sphere, had been satisfied. Viewed from the perspective of the lifeworld of those involved, therefore, the civil society of politically active citizens is inherently situated in this field of tension between the private and public spheres. As we shall see, the digitalization of public communication is blurring *the perception* of this boundary between the private and public spheres of life, although the social-structural prerequisites for this distinction, which also has far-reaching implications for the legal system, have not changed. From the perspective of the semi-private, semi-public spaces of communication in which users of social media are active today, the inclusive character of the public sphere, which was hitherto clearly separate from the private sphere, is disappearing. This constitutes, as I would now like to show, a disturbing development on the subjective side of media users that at the same time draws attention to the inadequacy of the political regulation of those new media.

(3) Before addressing specific changes in the structure of the media and hypotheses concerning their implications for the political function of the public sphere, I would like to interpolate some remarks on the economic, social and cultural boundary conditions that must be sufficiently satisfied if deliberative politics is to be possible. For it is only against the backdrop of the complex causes of the crisis tendencies of capitalist democracies in general that we can correctly assess the limited contribution, among the possible causes of an impairment of deliberative opinion and will formation, attributable to the digitalization of public communication.

Active citizenship requires, *first*, a by and large *liberal political culture* consisting of a delicate fabric of attitudes and taken-for-granted cultural assumptions. This is because the population's basic understanding of the democratic constitutional principles, which remains for the most part implicit, is embedded in an extensive network of historical memories and traditional beliefs, practices and value orientations; these are preserved from generation to generation only thanks to customary patterns of political socialization and institutionalized patterns of political education. The time span of half a century that was required, for example, for the political resocialization of the population of the (old) Federal Republic of Germany after the end of the Nazi dictatorship – despite the preceding 150 years of constitutional development – is an indicator of the obstacles that generally have to be overcome by any acclimatization to a liberal political culture. For the moral core of such a culture consists in the willingness of citizens to reciprocally recognize others as fellow citizens and democratic co-legislators endowed with equal rights.[16] This begins with regarding political adversaries in a spirit open to compromise as *opponents* and no longer as *enemies* – and it continues, beyond the limits of different ethnic, linguistic and religious forms of life, with the *reciprocal inclusion of strangers*, who wish to remain strangers to one another, in a shared political culture. This political culture must have differentiated itself from the respective majority culture to such an extent that every citizen in a pluralistic society can recognize himself or herself as a member. The social bond of a society, however heterogeneous it may be, will remain intact only if political integration as a general rule ensures a form of civic solidarity that, far from demanding unconditional altruism, calls for a limited reciprocal willingness to assist. This kind of solidarity [*Füreinander-Einstehen*] goes beyond the willingness to make compromises based on one's interests. Nevertheless, among fellow members of the same political community, it is invariably bound up with the indeterminate expectation of a reciprocal recon-ciliation of interests that may be required in the long run – specifically, with the expectation that others will feel obliged to provide similar assistance in a similar situation.[17] A 'liberal' political culture is not a breeding ground for 'libertarian' attitudes; it calls for an orientation to the common good, albeit one that makes modest demands on its addressees. An outvoted minority will not be able to accept majority decisions if all citizens base their electoral decisions *exclusively* on their short-term self-interest. A sufficient – and, moreover, *representative* – proportion of citizens must *also* be willing to perform the role of democratic co-legislators with an orientation to the common good.

A *second* precondition of an active civil society is a level of *social equality* that allows the spontaneous and sufficient participation of the electorate in the democratic process of opinion and will formation, although such participation must not be made compulsory. The architecture of the constitutional state's system of basic rights – which guarantees the *freedoms of private citizens* through subjective private rights (and welfare state entitlements), on the one hand, and the *political autonomy of public citizens* through subjective rights of public communication and participation, on the other – only becomes fully accessible in the light of the functional meaning of the complementary roles that the *private* and *public autonomy* of citizens also play for *each other*, aside from their respective intrinsic value. On the one hand, the political rights empower citizens in their civic role to participate in democratic legislation, which decides, among other things, on the distribution of private rights and entitlements, and thus on their opportunities to acquire an appropriate social status as private citizens; on the other hand, this societal status in turn creates the social presuppositions and motivations for the use that public citizens actually make of their civic rights in each case. There is ample evidence of the close correlation between social status and voter turnout. But this expectation that democratic participation and securing social status should enable each other will function only as long as democratic elections actually rectify substantial and structurally entrenched social inequalities. Empirical studies confirm that a vicious circle becomes established when *abstentionism* becomes *entrenched* among the lower status segments of the population due to resignation over the lack of perceptible improvements in living conditions. Then the political parties that used to be 'responsible' for the interests of these disadvantaged strata tend to neglect a clientele from which they cannot currently expect to receive votes; and this tendency in turn strengthens the motivation for abstentionism.[18] Today, the success of populist movements in mobilizing the potential of these non-voters is leading, not to a reversal, but to an ironic *inversion* of this vicious circle.[19] Then, of course, these radicalized groups of non-voters no longer participate in elections under the accepted *presuppositions* of a democratic election, but instead in the spirit of obstructionist 'opposition to the system'.[20] Even if this populism of the 'disconnected' cannot be explained solely by increasing social inequality, because other strata that are struggling to adapt to accelerated technological and social change also feel 'disconnected', it is at any rate a manifestation of a critical disintegration of society and a lack of successful policies to counteract it.[21]

This draws attention, finally, to the precarious relationship between the *democratic state* and a *capitalist economy*, which tends to reinforce social inequalities. The balancing of the conflicting functional imperatives by the welfare state is (at this level of abstraction) the *third precondition* for the success of a democratic regime worthy of the name. Political economy first revealed the systematic connection between the political system and society; this was the perspective from which I traced the structural transformation of the public sphere in the earlier work.[22] However, a liberal political culture is more a boundary condition for the state, one which happens to be satisfied to a greater or lesser extent, rather than something whose development could be influenced by the state itself with administrative means. The situation is different with the social stratification of society and the existing degree of social inequality.

In any case, self-perpetuating capitalist moderni-
zation generates a need for state regulation to curb the
centrifugal forces of social disintegration. The governments of those national welfare states that emerged in
the West during the second half of the twentieth century
find themselves compelled to undertake such political
countermeasures under increasingly demanding conditions of political legitimation. To avoid crises of social
integration, governments, as Claus Offe has shown, are
trying to satisfy two conflicting demands: on the one
hand, they must ensure sufficiently favourable conditions for the valorization of capital in order to generate
tax revenues; on the other hand, from the point of view
of political and social justice, governments must satisfy
the interest of the population as a whole in securing
the legal and material preconditions of the private and
public autonomy of every citizen – otherwise they will
be stripped of their democratic legitimacy. However,
capitalist democracies will only be able to steer a course
of crisis avoidance between these two imperatives if they
possess sufficient governance capacity. In other words,
the scope of the interventionist policies must match
the extent of the economic cycles relevant for securing
national prosperity. Evidently, the Western democracies
satisfied this condition sufficiently only for a limited
period – namely, only until the worldwide deregulation
of markets and the globalization of financial markets,

which since then have controlled the financial policies of the states.

A historical account of national public spheres based on these roughly outlined systematic viewpoints would reveal how difficult it is to arrive at any tenable generalizations at all about the framework conditions for the functioning of these public spheres in different historical periods. National peculiarities overlay the general trends towards the kind of nationally organized capitalism that shaped the post-war development of democracy in the West until the neoliberal turn. While during this period the development of the welfare state strengthened popular support for democracy, privatist trends towards depoliticization already emerged in the course of the development of a consumer society (whose beginnings I probably overemphasized in *Structural Transformation* in the climate of the Adenauer period, which was experienced as authoritarian). Since the shift towards neoliberal policies, however, the Western democracies have entered a phase of increasing internal destabilization, which is being aggravated by the challenges of the climate crisis and the growing pressure of immigration. A further aggravating factor is the perceived rise of China and of other 'emerging countries' and the resulting transformation of the global economic and political landscape. Domestically, social inequality has increased as nation-states' scope for action has been constrained by imperatives of globally deregulated markets. In the affected subcultures, the fear of social decline has grown in tandem with anxiety over the inability of the nation-state to cope with the complexity of the accelerated social changes.

Even apart from the new global political situation created by the pandemic, these circumstances suggest the prospect of closer integration for the nation-states united in the European Union – in other words, that they should strive to recover the competences they have lost at the national level in the course of this development by creating new political capacities for action at the transnational level.[23] However, a sober description of institutional approaches to global governance, which have consolidated rather than dismantled international asymmetries of power, does not inspire hope.[24] In particular, the indecisiveness of the EU in the face of its current problems raises the question of how nation-states can unite at the transnational level to form a democratic regime which, without itself assuming the character of an actual state, would nevertheless have the power to act globally. This would also presuppose a more pronounced *opening* of the national public spheres *to each other*. But both the divisions within the EU and the halting, but ultimately accomplished, Brexit suggest that existing democratic regimes are instead becoming depleted – and that the foreign policy of the major powers might even revert to a new kind of imperialism. For the time being, we do not know how the national and global economic problems facing a world society stricken by a pandemic will be perceived and processed by the political elites in our countries who still have some power to act. At the moment, there are few pointers for the desirable policy shift to a social and ecological agenda leading to greater integration at least of core Europe.

(4) The *media system* is of crucial importance for the role of the political public sphere in generating *competing public opinions* that satisfy the standards of deliberative politics. For the deliberative quality of public opinions depends on whether the process from which they emerge satisfies certain functional requirements on the input side and on the throughput and output sides. Public opinions are only *relevant* if opinion makers from the ranks of politics, as well as the lobbyists and PR agencies of the functional subsystems of society and, finally, the various actors from civil society, are *sufficiently responsive* to *discover* the problems in need of regulation and then to ensure the correct input. And public opinions are only *effective* if the corresponding topics and contributions of opinion makers find their way into the public eye and, on the output side, attract the attention of the wider – voting – population. Our

primary interest here is in the media system responsible for the throughput. Although for civil society
actors, *face-to-face encounters in everyday life* and in
public events represent the two *local regions of the public
sphere* in which their own initiatives originate, the *public
communication* steered by *mass media* is the only domain
in which the communicative din can condense into
relevant and effective public opinions. Our topic is
how digitalization has changed the media system that
steers this mass communication. The technically and
organizationally highly complex media system requires
a professionalized staff that plays the *gatekeeper role*
(as it has come to be called) for the communication
flows out of which the citizens distil public opinions.
This staff comprises journalists who work for the news
services, the media and the publishing houses – in
other words, specialists who perform authorial, editorial,
proofreading and managerial functions in the media and
publishing business. This staff directs the throughput
and, together with the companies that manage
production and organize distribution, forms the *infrastructure of the public sphere* that ultimately determines
the two decisive parameters of public communication
– the *scope* and the deliberative *quality* of the offerings.
How *inclusive* the reception of the *published* opinions
actually is – how *intensively* and with what investment
of time they are received on the output side by readers

and listeners and are *processed further* into effective public opinions in the two aforementioned local areas of the political public sphere and, finally, are cashed out in the political system in the currency of election results – ultimately depends on media users, specifically on their attention and interest, their time budgets, their educational background and so on.

The influence of digital media on a further structural transformation of the political public sphere can be read off, since the turn of the millennium or thereabouts, from the extent and nature of *media usage*. Whether this change also affects the *deliberative quality* of public debate is an open question. As the relevant research in the fields of communication studies, political science and the sociology of elections – especially research on voter turnout and public ignorance – demonstrates, the values for these two dimensions of public communication by democratic standards were already anything but satisfactory prior to digitalization; however, they pointed to democratic conditions that still fell some way short of stability-endangering crises. Today, the signs of political regression are there for everyone to see. Whether and to what extent the state of the political public sphere is also contributing to this development would have to be shown by examining the *inclusiveness* of public opinion formation and the *rationality* of the prominent public opinions. Evidently, empirical surveys of this second variable face major obstacles. While data exist for media usage, even in the case of procedurally regulated opinion formation in individual bodies, such as committees, parliaments and courts, it is difficult to operationalize a theoretical factor such as 'deliberative quality';[25] but the difficulty is even more acute in the case of the unregulated communication processes in large-scale national public spheres. However, the data from a long-term comparative study of media use enable us make inferences from an independent assessment of the quality of the media *offerings* that are being consumed to the level of reflectiveness of public opinions. Before pursuing this question further, however, we need to get clear about the revolutionary character of the new media. For they not only involve an expansion of the range of the previously available media, but also a caesura in the historical development of the media comparable to the introduction of printing.

After the first evolutionary advance to recording the spoken word in writing, the introduction of the mechanical printing press in early modernity meant that the alphabetic characters became detached from handwritten parchment; in recent decades, as a result of electronic digitalization, binary-coded characters have become detached in a similar way from printed paper. As this further, equally momentous innovation has unfolded, the communication flows of our garrulous species have spread, accelerated and become networked with unprecedented speed across the entire globe and, retrospectively, across all epochs of world history. With this global dissolution of spatial and temporal boundaries, these flows have simultaneously become *condensed*, their functions and contents have been *differentiated* and have *multiplied*, and they have been *generalized* across cultural and class-specific divisions. The innovative idea that ushered in this third revolution in communications technologies was the worldwide networking of computers, enabling any person to communicate with any other person regardless of where they were in the world. At first, it was scientists who used the new technology. In 1991, the American National Science Foundation decided to make this invention available for private use, which meant that it was also available for commercial purposes. This was the decisive step towards the establishment of the world wide web two years later, which created the technical basis for the logical completion of a development in communications technology that, over the course of human history, gradually overcame the original limitation of linguistic communication to face-to-face oral conversations and exchanges within hearing range. For many areas of life and activity, this innovation opens up undoubted advances. But for the democratic public sphere, the centrifugal expansion of simultaneously accelerated communication to include an arbitrary number of participants across arbitrary distances generates an ambivalent explosive force, because the public sphere, with its orientation to the centralized state organizations with the political power to act, is for the time being limited to national territories.[26] There can be no doubt that the expansion and acceleration of opportunities for communication and the increased scope of the publicly thematized events have advantages for political citizens as well. The world has also shrunk on the television screens in our living rooms. The contents of press products and of radio and television programmes do not change when they are received on smartphones. And when films are produced for streaming services like Netflix, this may lead to interesting aesthetic changes; but the changes in reception and the regrettable depletion of the cinema have long been heralded by the competition of television. Aside from its evident benefits, the new technology, on the other hand, also has highly ambivalent and potentially disruptive repercussions for the political public sphere in the national context. This is a result of how consumers of the new media make use of the availability of limitless possibilities for networking, i.e. of 'platforms' for possible communications with arbitrary addressees.

For the media structure of the public sphere, it is this platform character of the new media that represents the real novelty. It means that they dispense with the productive role of journalistic mediation and programme design performed by the old media; in this respect, the new media are not 'media' in the received sense. They radically alter the pattern of communication that has been dominant in the public sphere until now by *empowering* all potential users in principle to become independent and equally entitled authors. The 'new' media differ from their traditional counterparts in that digital companies make use of this technology to offer potential users the unlimited opportunities for digital networking like blank slates for their own communicative content. Unlike the traditional news services and publishers, such as print media, radio and television, these companies are not responsible for their own 'programmes', that is, for professionally produced and editorially filtered communicative contents. They neither produce, nor edit nor select; but by acting in the global network as intermediaries 'without responsibility' who establish new connections and, with the contingent multiplication and acceleration of unexpected contacts, initiate and intensify discourses with unpredictable contents, they are profoundly altering the character of public communication itself.

Broadcasting and publishing establish a linear and one-way connection between a broadcaster or publisher and many potential recipients. The two sides encounter each other in different roles: on the one side, publicly identifiable or known producers, editors and authors responsible for what they broadcast or publish; on the other side, an anonymous audience of readers, listeners or viewers. In contrast, platforms provide a multifaceted communicative connection open to networking that facilitates the spontaneous exchange of possible contents between potentially many users. The latter are not differentiated as regards their roles by the medium alone; rather, in communicative exchanges on spontaneously chosen topics, they encounter each other as participants who are in principle equal and self-responsible. Unlike the asymmetrical relationship between broadcasters or publishers and recipients, the decentralized connection between these media users is fundamentally reciprocal, but *its content is unregulated* because professional filters are lacking. The egalitarian and unregulated character of the relationships between participants and the equal authorization of users to make their own spontaneous contributions constitute the communicative pattern that was originally supposed to be the hallmark of the new media. Today, this great emancipatory promise is being drowned out, at least in part, by the desolate cacophony in fragmented, self-enclosed echo chambers.

The new pattern of communication has generated two remarkable effects for the structural transformation of the public sphere. At first, the egalitarian-universalistic claim of the bourgeois public sphere to include all citizens equally seemed to be finally fulfilled in the guise of the new media. These media promised to grant all citizens their own publicly perceptible voice and even to lend it mobilizing power. They would liberate users from the receptive role of addressees who choose between a limited range of programmes and give each individual the chance to make his or her voice heard in the anarchic exchange of spontaneous opinions. But the lava of this at once anti-authoritarian and egalitarian potential, which was still discernible in the Californian founding spirit of the early years, soon solidified in Silicon Valley into the libertarian grimace of world-dominating digital corporations. Moreover, the worldwide organizational potential offered by the new media is at the service of radical right-wing networks as well as the courageous Belarusian women in their tenacious protest against Lukashenko. One effect is the self-empowerment of media users; the other is the price the latter pay for being released from the editorial tutelage of the old media as long as they are not yet sufficiently proficient in dealing with the new media. Just as printing made everyone a potential reader, today digitalization is turning everyone into a potential author. But how long did it take until everyone was able to read?

The platforms do not offer their emancipated users any substitute for the professional selection and discursive examination of contents based on generally accepted cognitive standards. This is why there is currently so much talk of the erosion of the gatekeeper model of the mass media.[27] This model in no way implies the disenfranchisement of media users; it merely describes a form of communication that can enable citizens to acquire the necessary knowledge and information so that each of them can form his or her own opinion about problems in need of political regulation. A politically appropriate exercise of the author role, which is not the same as the consumer role, tends to heighten one's awareness of deficiencies in one's own level of knowledge. The author role also has to be learned; and as long as authorial competence is lacking in the political exchange in social media, the quality of the uninhibited discourses that are shielded from dissonant opinions and criticism will continue to suffer. This is what first exposes political opinion and will formation in the political community to the danger of *fragmentation* in conjunction with a simultaneously *unbounded* public sphere. The boundless communication networks that spontaneously take shape around certain topics or individuals can spread centrifugally while simultaneously condensing into communication circuits that dogmatically seal themselves off *from each other*. Then the trends towards fragmentation and the dissolution of boundaries reinforce each other to create a dynamic that counteracts the integrating power of the communication context of the nationally centred public spheres established by the press, radio and television. Before going into this dynamic in greater detail, I would first like to review how the share of social media in the overall media offerings has evolved.

(5) Empirically speaking, the impact of the introduction of the internet, and of social media in particular, on opinion and will formation in the political public sphere is not easy to circumscribe. However, the findings of the long-term study on media use in Germany conducted by the national broadcasters for the period from 1964 to 2020 permit some rough conclusions about changes in the media offerings and their use.[28] There was a considerable *expansion* of *offerings*, first as a result of the introduction of commercial television, and then above all due to the wide range of online options. This holds not only for the national level, since the internet also makes a large number of 'foreign' press offerings and radio and television programmes available. Interested people from around the world were able to watch the storming of the Capitol live on CNN. Correspondingly, the time budget invested in daily media consumption has absolutely exploded. The amount of time spent using all media has risen sharply since 2000, but peaked in 2005; since then, it has levelled off at a saturation point of an astounding eight hours a day. The proportions of the

time devoted to the different media have shifted over the decades. Since 1970, the utilization of the then-new medium of television overtook that of the traditional media of daily newspapers and radio. But even after the impact of the online competition became clearly felt from 2000 onwards, television and radio have continued to maintain the greatest reach. Book consumption also remained quite stable, with fluctuations, between 1980 and 2015. What must be emphasized in our context is that, in contrast, the corresponding reach of daily newspapers underwent a steady decline since the introduction of television, from 69 per cent of the daily time budget in 1964 to 33 per cent in 2015. The slump since the introduction of new media is reflected in the dramatic decline in the reach of printed newspapers and magazines from 60 per cent in 2005 to 22 per cent in 2020. This trend is destined to continue at an accelerated rate, given that 40 per cent of people in the age group of 14- to 29-year-olds were still reading printed newspapers or magazines in 2005, compared with 6 per cent in the same age group in 2020. At the same time, the reading intensity has decreased: while the average reader spent 38 minutes per day reading newspapers in 1980 (and 11 minutes reading magazines), the average daily reading time decreased to 23 minutes in 2015 (or 11 minutes for magazines), and to 15 minutes in 2020 (for newspapers and magazines combined). Of course, newspaper consumption has also shifted to the internet; but aside from the fact that reading digitalized texts presumably does not demand the same level of intensive attention and analytical processing as reading printed texts, alternative online information offerings (podcasts, for example, or news portals) cannot fully compensate for the offerings of daily newspapers. An indicator of this is the average time spent reading digital texts each day factored across the population as a whole – 18 minutes in total, 6 minutes of which are spent on newspapers and magazines.

The most recent representative Eurobarometer of the populations of the then 28 EU countries, which was conducted at the end of 2019, confirms the current scale of the offerings and the utilization of the various media: on a daily basis, 81 per cent of respondents use television, 67 per cent the internet in general, 47 per cent social media, 46 per cent radio and 26 per cent the press, whereas the proportion of daily newspaper readers in 2010 was still 38 per cent. The Eurobarometer records daily utilization of social media separately from that of the internet in general, and this share has risen astonishingly rapidly, from 18 per cent of all respondents in 2010 to 48 per cent currently. Interestingly, television and, at a lower level, radio are also maintaining their leading role in the demand for 'political information on national affairs'. For political information, 77 per cent of those surveyed name television, 40 per cent radio and 36 per cent the print media as their 'main sources', while 49 per cent cite the internet in general and 20 per cent social media. The fact that this last figure, which is of interest in the present context, has already risen by a further four points compared to the previous year's survey confirms the increasing trend also documented elsewhere. In any case, the drastic decline in the consumption of daily newspapers and magazines is also an indicator that, since the introduction of the internet, the average amount of attention paid to political news and the analytical processing of politically relevant issues have declined. Nonetheless, the relative stability of the share of television and radio also in general media consumption suggests that, for the time being, these two media are providing reliable and sufficiently diverse political information to at least three-quarters of the electorate in the EU member states.

This makes another trend all the more striking. Evidently, the increasing infiltration of the political public sphere by fake news, and in particular the spectacular development towards a 'post-truth democracy' that became the alarming normality in the US under the Trump administration, have also reinforced distrust in the media *in Europe*. Forty-one per cent of the respondents to the Eurobarometer survey doubt that the reporting of the national media is free from political and economic influence; 39 per cent explicitly affirm this distrust with regard to the public media that today form the backbone of a liberal public sphere; and as many as 79 per cent claim that they have encountered distorted or false news.

These data provide information about the quantitative changes in the spectrum of available media and their utilization; however, they only provide indirect evidence of the quality of the public opinions formed on this basis and of the extent of citizens' involvement in the process of opinion and will formation. Therefore, I must confine myself to informed conjectures. On the one hand, the dramatic loss of relevance of the print media compared to the dominant audio-visual media seems to point to a decline in the level of aspiration of the offerings. Hence, it also seems to indicate that the citizens' receptiveness and intellectual processing of politically relevant news and problems are on the decline. Incidentally, this diagnosis is confirmed by how the politically leading daily and weekly newspapers have adjusted their offerings to the 'colourful' format of entertaining Sunday newspapers. On the other hand, as a participant observer one finds daily evidence that the remaining more sophisticated national newspapers and magazines continue to serve as the leading political media that specify the reflected contributions and positions on the agenda-setting topics for the other media, especially television. However, mistrust in the truth, seriousness and completeness of the programmes is increasing among the general population in Germany, even though it can be assumed that the public broadcasters continue to ensure a reliable supply of news and political programmes. The growing doubts about the quality of the state-financed media presumably go hand in hand with the increasingly widespread conviction that the political class is either unreliable or corrupt, or at any rate suspect. This general picture suggests that, on the one hand, the diversity of the media on the supply side and a corresponding pluralism of opinions, arguments and perspectives on life fulfil important preconditions for the long-term formation of critical opinions that are immune to prejudice; but that, on the other hand, the increasing dissonance of diverse voices and the complexity of the challenging topics and positions are leading a growing minority of media consumers to use digital platforms to retreat into shielded echo chambers of the like-minded. For the digital platforms not only invite their users to spontaneously generate intersubjectively confirmed worlds of their own, they also at the same time seem to lend the stubborn internal logic of these islands of communication the *epistemic status of competing public spheres*. But before we can assess this subjective side of the changes in recipients' attitudes due to the media offerings, we must first examine the economic dynamics that are increasingly distorting subjective perceptions of the editorial public sphere. For the idiosyncratic character of these modes of reception promoted by social media should not blind us to the economic anchoring of the – for the time being largely politically unregulated – transformation of the structure of the media that we have roughly outlined.

(6) To describe the platforms as 'media offerings for networking communicative contents across arbitrary distances' is, if not naïve, at least incomplete, in view of the far from neutral performance of algorithm-steered platforms such as Facebook, YouTube, Instagram and Twitter. For these actually existing new media are companies that obey the imperatives of capital valor-ization and, measured by their market capitalization, are among the 'most valuable' corporations worldwide. They generate their profits by exploiting data, which they sell for advertising purposes or otherwise as commodities. These data consist of information that accrues as a by-product of their user-oriented offerings in the form of the personal data their customers leave behind on the internet (now subject to their formal consent). Newspapers are also generally privately owned companies that are financed to a large extent by advertising revenue. But while the old media are

themselves the advertising vehicles, the kind of value creation that has provoked criticism of 'surveillance capitalism'[29] feeds on commercially exploitable information that is randomly 'snagged' by *other* services and in turn enables individualized advertising strategies.[30] Through these processes steered by algorithms, social media are also promoting a further advance in the commodification of lifeworld contexts.

However, I am interested in a different aspect, namely the pressure to adjust being exerted on the old media by the valorization logic of the new media. The old media are suitable vehicles for advertising only as long as their contents are commercially successful. However, these contents themselves obey a completely different inherent logic – namely, the demand for texts and programmes whose form and content must satisfy cognitive, normative or aesthetic standards. That readers and audiences evaluate journalistic performances according to such epistemic standards (broadly understood) becomes immediately apparent once we grasp – from the philosophical perspective of analysis of the lifeworld – the important function that the media fulfil in providing orientation in the increasingly confusing 'media society'. In the face of societal complexity, the media are the intermediary which, given the diverse perspectives presented by social situations and cultural forms of life, sifts out an intersubjectively shared core from among the competing interpretations of the world and validates it as generally *rationally accepted.* Of course, daily or weekly newspapers, with their classic threefold division of contents into politics, business and feature pages, are never the *final* authority regarding the truth or correctness of individual statements or recognized interpretations of facts, the plausibility of general assessments, or even the soundness of standards or procedures of judgement. But with their daily stream of new information and interpretations, the media constantly confirm, correct and supplement the blurred everyday image of a *presumptively objective world,* which more or less *all contemporaries* assume is also accepted by everyone else as 'normal' or valid.

Why the advance towards the 'platformization of the public sphere' is creating difficulties for the traditional media, both economically and in view of dwindling journalistic influence and the adjustment of professional standards, is explained by Otfried Jarren and Renate Fischer.[31] Since there is a correlation between circulation and advertising revenues, the decline in demand for printed newspapers and magazines is jeopardizing the economic basis of the press; and thus far it has not found a really successful business model for commercial sales of digital formats, since on the internet it faces competition from providers who offer their users corresponding information free of charge. The result is cutbacks and precarious employment conditions with negative effects on the quality and scope of editorial work. But the losses in the advertising and audience stakes are not the only factors that are weakening the relevance and interpretive power of the press. Adjusting to the online competition calls for changes in how journalists work. Even if the 'audience turn' – i.e. the greater involvement of the audience and an increased sensitivity to the reactions of readers – is not necessarily detrimental, the trends towards deprofessionalization and an understanding of journalistic work as a neutral, depoliticized service are intensifying. When data and attention management replace targeted research and precise interpretation, 'newsrooms, previously places of political debate, are transformed into coordination centres for sourcing and managing the production and distribution of content'.[32] The change in professional standards is a reflection of how the press, which has the greatest inherent affinity for the discursive character of opinion and will formation by *citizens*, is adjusting to the commercial services of the platforms that are soliciting the attention of *consumers*. With the triumph of the imperatives of the attention economy, however, the new media are also intensifying the trends, long familiar from the tabloid and popular press, towards entertainment, emotionalization and the personalization of the issues of concern for the political public sphere.

With the alignment of political programmes with offers of entertainment and consumption addressed to the citizens as consumers, we touch on trends towards depoliticization that have been observed in media research since the 1930s, but which are evidently intensifying as a result of the offerings of social media. It is only when we turn our attention away from the objective side of the expanded media structure and its altered economic basis towards the side of the recipients and their altered modes of reception that we broach the central question of whether social media are changing how their users perceive the political public sphere. Of course, the technical advantages of commercial platforms, and even of a medium like Twitter that compels its users to produce concise messages, offer the users undoubted benefits for political, professional and private purposes. But these advances are not our topic. Our question is rather whether these platforms are also prompting a kind of exchange about implicit or explicit political views that, through the changed mode of use, could influence *how the political public sphere is perceived as such*. With a view to the subjective side of the use of the new media, Philipp Staab and Thorsten Thiel refer to Andreas Reckwitz's theory of the 'society of singularities' and, in particular, to the incentives that the activating platforms provide their users for narcissistic self-promotion and the 'staging of singularity'.[33] If we make a clear distinction between 'individualization' – i.e. the distinctiveness a person acquires through her life history – and 'singularization' – i.e. the visibility and gain in distinction she can achieve through spontaneous contributions on the internet – then the 'promise of singularization' may be the correct term for influencers who court the approval of followers for their own programme and reputation. Be that as it may, when it comes to the contribution of social media to opinion and will formation in the political public sphere, a different aspect of reception seems more important to me. It has often been observed that the spontaneously self-directed and fragmented public spheres that split off both from the editorial or official public sphere and from one another generate a pull towards self-referential reciprocal confirmation of interpretations and opinions. If participants' experiences and perceptions of what were hitherto called publicness and the political public sphere were to change, affecting the customary conceptual *distinction between private and public spheres*, this would necessarily have far-reaching consequences for the self-understanding of internet consumers as citizens. For the moment we lack the data to test this hypothesis; but the indications prompting such a hypothesis are troubling enough.

The societal basis for the legal and political differentiation of the public sphere from the private sphere of economic, civil society and familial activity has not undergone any structural change during the period under consideration; for the capitalist economic system is itself based on this separation. In constitutional democracies, this structure has also found a reflection in the consciousness of citizens. And their perception is the crucial issue. Citizens are expected to make their political decisions in the field of tension between self-interest and the orientation towards the common good. As we have seen, this tension is played out in the communicative space of a political public sphere that as a matter of principle includes all citizens as a potential audience. The very fact that public flows of communication pass through editorial sluices sets them apart from all private and business contacts. Different standards apply to the composition of print products addressed to an anonymous reading public than to private correspondence, which for a long time was still written by hand.[34] What is constitutive for the public sphere is not the disparity between active and passive participation in discourse, but rather the topics that deserve *shared* interest, as well as the professional processing and rationality of the contributions that promote mutual understanding about shared and diverse interests. We should not overstrain the spatial metaphorics of the distinction between private and public 'spaces'; what is decisive is the perception of the (politically contested) *threshold* between private matters and the public issues discussed in the political public sphere. This perception is also shared by the social movements that create counterpublics to combat the narrowing of vision of the media public. Apart from the substantive reference to the central political authority with the power to act, it is the form and relevance of the selected editorial contributions that attract the attention of the audience. And this expectation concerning the reliability, quality and general relevance of public contributions is also constitutive for perceptions of the inclusive character of a public sphere that is supposed to direct the attention of *all* citizens to the *same* topics, in order to stimulate each of them to make their *own* judgements in accordance with the recognized standards about the issues of relevance for political decision-making.[35]

It is true that, since the emergence of 'media societies', the societal basis for such a separation of the public sphere from the private spheres of life has not undergone any essential changes. Nonetheless, the more or less exclusive use of social media may have led in parts of the population to a change in the *perception of the public sphere* that has blurred the distinction between 'public' and 'private', and thus the inclusive meaning of the public sphere. In the literature in communication studies, one increasingly encounters observations of a trend away from traditional perceptions of the political public sphere and of politics itself.[36] In certain subcultures, the public sphere is no longer perceived as being inclusive, and the political public sphere is no longer seen as a space of communication for a generalization of interests that includes all citizens. Therefore, I will try to explain a hypothesis and render it plausible as such.[37] As mentioned, the internet opens up virtual spaces in which users can empower themselves as authors in a new way. Social media create freely accessible public spaces that invite all users to make interventions which are not checked by anyone – and which, as it happens, have also long since enticed politicians to exert direct personalized influence on the voting public. This plebiscitary 'public sphere', which has been stripped down to 'like' and 'dislike' clicks, rests on a technical and economic infrastructure. But in these freely accessible media spaces, all users who are, as it were, released from the need to satisfy the entry requirements of the editorial public sphere and, from their point of view, have been freed from 'censorship', can in principle address an anonymous public and solicit its approval. These spaces seem to acquire a peculiar anonymous intimacy: according to hitherto valid standards, they can be understood *neither as public nor as private*, but most readily as a sphere of communication that had previously been reserved for private correspondence but has now been inflated into a new and intimate kind of public sphere.

Users empowered as authors provoke attention with their messages, because the unstructured public sphere is first *created* by the comments of readers and the 'likes' of followers. To the extent that this leads to the formation of self-sustaining echo chambers, these bubbles share with the classical form of publicness their porousness to *further* networking; at the same time, however, they differ from the fundamentally inclusive character of the public sphere – and from the corresponding contrast to the private – in their resistance to dissonant and their assimilating inclusion of consonant voices into their own *limited, identity-preserving* horizon of supposed, yet professionally unfiltered, 'knowledge'. From a point of view fortified by the mutual confirmation of users' judgements, claims to universality extending beyond their own horizons become suspect in principle of hypocrisy. From the limited perspective of such a *semi-public sphere*, the political public sphere of constitutional democracies loses the appearance of an inclusive space for a possible discursive clarification of competing claims to truth and a general equal consideration of interests; precisely this public sphere, which hitherto *presented itself as inclusive,* is then downgraded to one of the semi-public spheres that compete on an equal footing.[38] One symptom of this is the *twofold strategy* of spreading fake news while simultaneously combating the 'lying press', which in turn unsettles the public and the leading media themselves.[39] But when the shared space of 'the political' degenerates into the battleground of competing publics, the democratically legitimized political programmes pushed through by the state provoke conspiracy theories – as in the case of the anti-Corona demonstrations, which were staged in a libertarian spirit while in fact being driven by authoritarian motives. These tendencies can already be observed in member states of the European Union; but they can even grip and deform the political system as such, if it has been undermined and riven long enough by social-structural conflicts. In the United States, politics was drawn into the maelstrom of a persistent polarization of the public sphere after the administration and large sections of the ruling party accommodated itself to the self-perception of a president who was successful on social media and obtained the daily plebi-scitary approval of his populist following on Twitter.[40] The – we can only hope, temporary – disintegration of the political public sphere was reflected in the fact that, for almost half the population, communicative contents could no longer be exchanged in the currency of criticizable validity claims. The significant factor for a widespread *distortion of the perception of the political public sphere* is not the accumulation of fake news, but the fact that fake news can no longer even be identified as such.[41]

In communication studies and social science, it is now commonplace to speak of disrupted public spheres that have become detached from the journalistically institutionalized public sphere. But scholarly observers would be mistaken to conclude that the description of these symptomatic phenomena should be separated from questions of democratic theory altogether.[42] After all, communication in semi-public spheres that have become independent is by no means depoliticized; and even where that is the case, the power of this communication to shape the worldviews of those involved is not apolitical. It is harmful for a democratic system as a whole when the infrastructure of the public sphere is no longer able to direct the citizens' attention to the relevant issues that need to be decided or to ensure the formation of competing public opinions – and that means, *qualitatively filtered* opinions. If we recall the complex preconditions for the survival of inherently crisis-prone capitalist democracies, it is indeed clear that there may be deeper reasons for a loss of function of the political public sphere. But that does not exempt us from looking for *obvious* reasons.

I see one such reason in the coincidence of the emergence of Silicon Valley, i.e. the commercial use of the digital network, on the one hand, and the global spread of the neoliberal economic programme, on the other. The globally expanded zone of free flows of communication originally made possible by the invention of the technical structure of the 'net' presented itself as the mirror image of an ideal market. This market did not first have to be deregulated. In the meantime, however, this suggestive image is being disrupted by the algorithmic control of communication flows that is feeding the concentration of market power of the large internet corporations. The skimming and digital processing of customers' personal data, which are more or less inconspicuously exchanged for the information provided free of charge by search engines, news portals and other services, explains why the EU Competition Commissioner would like to regulate this market. But competition law is the wrong lever if one's aim is to correct the fundamental flaw that platforms, unlike traditional media, do not want to accept liability for the dissemination of truth-sensitive, and hence deception-prone, communicative contents. The fact that the press, radio and television, for example, are obliged to correct false reports draws attention to the circumstance of interest in the present context. Because of the special nature of their goods, which are not mere commodities, the platforms cannot evade all duties of journalistic due diligence.

They, too, are responsible and should be liable for news that they neither produce nor edit; for this information also has the power to shape opinions and mentalities. Most importantly, it is not governed by the quality standards of commodities but by the cognitive standards of judgements without which neither the objectivity of the world of facts nor the identity and commonality of our intersubjectively shared world are possible for us.[43] In a hard-to-imagine 'world' of fake news that was no longer identifiable as such – i.e. a world in which fake news was indistinguishable from true information – no child would be able to grow up without developing clinical symptoms. Therefore, maintaining a media structure that enables the inclusiveness of the public sphere and the deliberative character of public opinion and will formation is not a matter of political preference but a constitutional imperative.

Deliberative Democracy: An Interview

Today many theorists of deliberation stress that deliberative standards, such as the standard of equal power in the aggregative model of democracy, function as 'regulative ideals'. This implies that the oft-quoted concept of the 'ideal speech situation' is not ultimately a practically achievable goal. Do you see this as a welcome development?

Your question provides me with an opportunity to clarify a persistent misunderstanding about the concept 'ideal speech situation'. Aside from the fact that I have not used this misleading expression since my 1972 essay on 'Theories of Truth'[1] and have long since revised it, one must take into account the context in which a concept is introduced. At the time I used the expression to refer to the cluster of pragmatic presuppositions that we *must* assume *as a matter of fact* whenever we engage in argumentation about the validity of propositions. As participants in discourse, we 'know' that we are not arguing 'seriously' if coercion or manipulation is at work in such an exchange of reasons, or if some of those affected are excluded or if relevant opinions and positions are suppressed. We must *presuppose* that only the unforced force of the better argument comes into play in the given situation. This knowledge of ours, our knowledge of *how* to participate in a rational discourse, has a regulating influence on how participants actually behave when arguing, even when they are aware that they can fulfil these pragmatic presuppositions only approximately. In view of this counterfactual status, one can perhaps say that the *idealizing content* of the pragmatic presuppositions of discourse plays the role of a regulative idea for the participants. From the *observer perspective*, one will find that rational discourses rarely occur in pure form. However, this in no way alters the fact that, from the *participant perspective*, we must make those presuppositions that are constitutive of the cooperative search for truth. This is shown, among other things, by the fact that we appeal to these very standards when we criticize a mere pretence of engaging in discourse or an agreement reached by dubious means.

When a philosopher examines the concept of rational discourse, he adopts the epistemic stance of a participant and attempts to reconstruct the latter's performative 'knowledge of how to engage in argument', and hence tries to convert it into explicit '*knowledge of what* …'. By contrast, a social scientist studying discourses – for example, reflecting on democratic practice – is concerned not with rational discourse as such. Rather, she approaches these phenomena from an observer's perspective, describes discourses in space and time – that is, in their diverse empirical manifestations – and for this purpose favours the less sharply defined concept of 'deliberation'. But an empirical researcher also has good reasons not to casually disregard the participants' performative knowledge.[2]

There are many practices that can function only as long as the participants make certain idealizing assumptions. In a constitutional democracy, for example, citizens will conduct their disputes through the courts only as long as they can assume that more or less fair rulings are to be expected (and do not let themselves be perturbed by the evidence unearthed by 'realists' or the advocates of Critical Legal Studies that judges' motives are guided by interests). Similarly, citizens will participate in political elections only as long as they are able to assume implicitly that their voice can make itself heard and that their vote 'counts' – it should even have the same weight as every other vote. These are also idealizing presuppositions. Unlike informal discourses, however, these discursive practices, which are embedded in institutions of the state, can lose their credibility. Voters who feel 'disconnected' stop going to the polls.

Democratic elections cease to function properly, for example, when the failure to take seriously the interests of underprivileged non-voters leads to a vicious circle, or when the infrastructures of public communication disintegrate to such an extent that numbing resentment gains the upper hand over well-informed public opinions. In short, I do not see deliberative politics as an aloof ideal against which sordid reality must be measured, but as an existential presupposition of any democracy worthy of the name.

It is not a historical accident that a bourgeois public sphere developed in tandem with liberal democracy. Also under the changed conditions of mass democracy, parliamentary legislation, competition between political parties and free political elections need to be rooted in a vibrant political public sphere, an active civil society and a liberal political culture. Without this societal context, the essential deliberative presuppositions for democratic legitimation of rule lack any foothold in reality.

Many theorists of deliberation object that consensus is not necessarily the goal of a successful process of deliberation; rather, deliberation can also lead only to the clarification of preferences. Does the assumed orientation to reaching understanding exercise too strong an influence on deliberation?

Let me make the following clear in advance: the assumption that political discourses are also oriented to the goal of reaching an agreement in no way implies an idealizing 'idyllic' conception of the democratic process as a convivial university seminar. On the contrary, it is safe to assume that it is precisely the participants' orientation to the truth or rightness of their beliefs that first adds fuel to the fire of political disputes and lends them a polemical character. To argue is to contradict. But it is only the right – and, indeed, the encouragement – to say 'no' to each other that elicits the epistemic potential of language without which we could not *learn from one another*. And this is the point of deliberative politics, namely, that by engaging in political disputes, we improve our beliefs and thereby approach the correct solution to problems. This presupposes, of course, that the political process has an epistemic dimension in the first place ...

Do you think that the clarification of preferences represents a fully valid goal of deliberation? And can deliberation also produce results that cannot be described as consensus in the strict sense, such as compromises or win-win situations?

Clarifying preferences is, of course, the first step in every political discourse; at the same time, discourses justify the expectation that the parties should *examine* their initial preferences in the course of deliberation and also *change* them in the light of better reasons. This condition enables us to distinguish cases of deliberative opinion and will formation from compromises. Discourses have an epistemic dimension because they create room for *arguments to exert their preference-altering force*, whereas compromises, which are negotiated between power-wielding partners in the currency of reciprocal concessions or shared benefits, leave existing preferences unaffected. Both discourses and bargaining are legitimate ways of reaching political agreements. One must pay attention to the kind of issue under discussion in order to establish whether an agreement should be sought along the epistemic paths of discourse or via the route of negotiation.

The crucial question, however, is *what kind of reasons* we think are sufficiently forceful to bring about rationally motivated changes in preferences. The answer depends on philosophical background assumptions about which political scientists who conduct empirical research on deliberative politics also have to achieve clarity. Empiricists defend a non-cognitivist conception of practical reason that is supposed to be restricted to the capacity for rational choice and to making strategic

decisions. According to this conception, one's preferences can be influenced exclusively by better information
about scopes for action and risks and by comparatively more reliable calculations of the consequences
of possible alternative courses of action; however, they
cannot be changed by *taking the preferences of other
participants into consideration*. This restrictive view is
counter-intuitive, because the reasons in terms of which
we argue about the rightness of binding norms of action,
or about which values are preferable, carry no less
epistemic weight in the rationally motivated formation
of preferences than information about facts.

Political discourses deal not only with the truth of
descriptive propositions but also with validity claims that
we associate with normative and evaluative propositions.
Thus the justice of a legal norm can be examined from
the moral viewpoint by asking, with regard to a matter
in need of regulation, whether it is 'equally good' for all
concerned; here a principle of universalization comes
into play. The members of a political community can,
furthermore, examine a decision between competing
values by asking which of these values is preferable in
the light of the ethos of the community's shared form
of life. By contrast, preferences as such are not in need
of justification, because such first-person statements are
authorized by each individual's privileged access to her
own desires. Problems of justice are understood as a

cognitive task, whereas decisions concerning the priority of some values over others can be regarded as calling for a process of rationally motivated will formation that is in part cognitive and in part volitional. In each case, the participants' orientation to reaching a consensus follows from the meaning of the respective issues. Unlike preferences, norms and values never concern only a single person.

On the other hand, of course, the required orientation of participants towards consensus, which is *presupposed* with the epistemic understanding of discourse, does not mean that those involved tend to have the unrealistic expectation that they will actually achieve a consensus on political questions. Practical discourses require their participants to demonstrate an improbable willingness to adopt each other's perspectives and to orient themselves to generalizable interests or shared values. After all, this is why the democratic process connects deliberations subject to time constraints with majority decisions. The majoritarian principle (whether it is a question of a simple or a qualified majority) can be justified in turn by the discursive character of opinion formation. Assuming that the presumption of rationally acceptable results is justified and the decision is reversible, each outvoted minority, given the prospect of a resumption of discourse, can subject itself to the will of the majority without having to abandon its own position.

The theory of communicative action assumes that strategic intentions undermine the deliberative orientation to reaching understanding. In other words, truly deliberative actors must bring an orientation to reaching understanding to discourse. In politics, on the other hand, strategic orientations on the part of actors play a central role, which raises the question of whether the deliberative model can have any relevance in political decision-making processes.

Well, most political decisions are, of course, the result of compromises. But modern democracies combine popular sovereignty with the rule of law, which means that compromise formation takes place within the framework of constitutional norms. Such a constitutional framework means that the search for compromises is consistently connected with questions of political justice and of the realization of values that enjoy political priority. And because these questions imbue political deliberation with an epistemic meaning, deliberation cannot be restricted from the outset to compromises over the distribution of goods between self-interested negotiation partners. Interesting hybrid forms exist and they have been analysed by Mark E. Warren and Jane Mansbridge. They discuss, among others, the example of climate policy legislation that makes use of tradable emission credits.[3] Although in this example a compromise is reached between the climate policy objectives of emission control and the interests of the affected companies, this compromise also touches on questions of justice because it takes into account a policy goal that had already been adopted – namely, putting a stop to global climate change as soon as possible in the general interest of citizens and future generations.

In political theory, the opposition between strategic and communicative action has opened the door for agonistic theories (e.g. that of Chantal Mouffe) that claim to be 'more political' than deliberative theory.

Theories that start from a certain concept of 'the' political do not go far enough, regardless of whether they defend an agonistic concept of political struggle, a systemic concept of administratively steered power, or a communicative concept of interactively generated power. If we look back at the evolutionary origins of state formation, it is evident that political power is co-original with state-sanctioned laws. As a result, those early societies acquired the reflexive capacity to intentionally influence their own conditions of life through collectively binding decisions. Originally, the belief of subjects in the legitimacy of political power grounded in the sacred complex was a precondition of the stability of existing political systems, although, since the 'axial' period, more exacting standards of legitimacy became a source of criticism of political power as well. Following the secularization of state power in the modern era, finally, democratically generated constitutions superseded religion in this role of provider of legitimacy. Since then, the widespread background consensus on constitutional principles among the population generally differs from a religiously based legitimation in virtue of being brought about democratically – hence, also through the deliberative exchange of arguments. Such a background consensus must be tacitly renewed in every generation, for otherwise democracies would not endure.

However, the fact that this background consensus has a *non-antagonistic core* does not mean that the constitution organizes the democratic process as a procedure that is *continuously* oriented to consensus – far from it. One must start from the different functions that political communication is supposed to fulfil in different ways in different arenas with its contributions to a democratic process that *is as a whole filtered through deliberation*. Then the interesting differences between the functionally necessary requirements of rationality in the various arenas become apparent. These requirements become more and more lax across the various levels of political communication – ranging from, at one extreme, the comparatively high rational requirements of *legally institutionalized* discourses within the courts and parliamentary bodies to, at the other, the disputes between political actors *in the public sphere* directed *to a diffuse audience,* the election campaigns, the voices within civil society and, in general, the political mass communication conveyed by the media. For example, the agonistic character of election campaigns, conflicts between opposing political parties, and confrontations between protest movements and the establishment can be correctly assessed only if one recognizes that the functional contribution of political mass communication to a by and large deliberative process of opinion and will formation is that of generating competing public opinions on topics relevant for decision-making.

An orientation to consensus is functionally required only in the deliberations of those institutions in which legally binding decisions are made. The informal communication within the wider public sphere can also withstand robust protests or wild forms of conflict, because their contribution is limited to mobilizing the relevant themes, information and arguments, whereas decisions are taken elsewhere. Nothing more may be needed to spark an antagonistic dynamic within the public sphere than the conflict-generating orientation to truth that citizens associate with their expressions of political opinions. But that also tends to be functional in generating competing public opinions.

In this context, how do you assess the thesis, which is increas-ingly often defended, that good and desirable deliberation should include not only rational reasons (or justifications) but also narratives, emotions and rhetoric?

Here again one must view the picture as a whole. The form of mass communication from which the politi-cally relevant public opinions are supposed to emerge is indeed largely fuelled by inputs from the side of the government, the political parties and interest groups, which are then processed by the media. As a general rule, civil society actors have a tough time when faced with the political parties and the experts, PR agencies and lobbies of the various functional subsystems. On the other hand, civil society is the only society-wide sounding board for the problems and impositions caused by malfunctioning subsystems that are troubling their respective clients or 'consumers', as it were. Therefore, the communicative network of civil society plays the role of a kind of early-warning system for politics that registers critical experiences from private areas of life, processes them into voices of protest and feeds them into the political public sphere. Since the social movements into which protest may condense are not the norm, the unedited 'offstage' voices from civil society, when faced with the well-formulated pronouncements of the other political actors, can gain a hearing more readily the more spontaneously they are expressed. Narratives have an intelligible propositional content, as do the passions and desires to which they give expression; moreover, a forceful rhetoric is still among the more conventional means on the long path that a theme must follow to attracting sufficient media attention and finding its way onto the agenda of some influential agency. Spectacular, even transgressive, actions can also facilitate messages that are intended to 'arrive' in the political system.

Some theorists of deliberation emphasize, furthermore, that self-interest should also be part of deliberation (in addition to considerations of the common good), albeit with the proviso that individual interests are legitimate only when constrained by principles of fairness. How do you assess this argument? Are individual interests an essential aspect of desirable deliberation?

I regard this as self-evident. Even moral discourse must start from the interests of the individual parties to the conflict before one can ask from the perspective of justice what is in the equal interest of all affected. To be sure, no democratic polity can function properly when its citizens, in their role as national citizens and co-legislators, follow their own interests *exclusively*. John Rawls rightly associates the 'public use of reason' with the expectation that citizens should exhibit political virtues. On the other hand, one must also insist against Rousseau that the democratic state can make only modest demands on its citizens when it comes to adopting an orientation to the common good.

How tightly is deliberative democracy integrated into a modern liberal form of political culture? In other words: Can deliberation function at the global level? And, if so, would you agree that this also means that deliberative standards must be adjusted to different cultures?

We must at any rate be on our guard against overexuberant notions that democracy can be simply exported without further ado, whether peacefully or by military force. Liberal democracy is such a demanding and fragile form of government because it can be realized only in and through the heads of its citizens. On the other hand, this does not mean that, at the international level, 'the West', if I may speak in such terms, should relativize the claim to universality it raises for principles of the democratic rule of law. What is at stake in this discussion are *rational principles* not *contestable values*. The idle talk about 'our values' that supposedly have to be defended against the values of other cultures is precisely what polarizes the international community. As a philosopher, I defend the view that 'we' have good reasons in intercultural discourse to defend the universal validity of human rights as the moral foundations of constitutional democracy. However, this is subject to the condition that 'we' participate in such discourses with a *willingness to learn* and as *one party among others*. Willingness to learn is already called for by the fact that the brutally violent history of Western imperialism has taught us that we must let our eyes be opened by other cultures concerning the blind spots in our interpretation and application of human rights not only in the past but also in the present. But even the presumptive universal validity of the principles now enshrined in the UN Charter does not mean that we may conduct crusades to disseminate liberal democracy. For the reasons you imply with your question, a democratic system imposed by paternalistic means cannot achieve long-term stability.

On the other hand, I also think that the so-called second-best solution of 'adapting' principles to the values and circumstance of a foreign culture is wrong. The well-meaning 'political' way of dealing with principles of political justice, as recommended, for example, by John Rawls in *The Law of Peoples*, also forces one to adopt a dubious paternalistic attitude towards other civilizations.

In some social and political situations – for example, under conditions of deep religious or ethnic divisions or when participants do not trust each other – deliberative ideals such as argumentative rationality or respect are difficult to implement. What role, if any, can deliberative theory play in such situations?

Perhaps we should first recall that, as our societies become more pluralistic, the burden of social integration shifts from the level of local forms of life and national cultures to the state and politics. Among the major reasons for this shift are the accelerated changes in living conditions caused by technology and, above all, increasing immigration from foreign cultures. Aside from the common language or languages, what all citizens of a political community are expected to share increasingly crystallizes around citizenship status. Therefore, the political culture can no longer coincide with the traditional majority culture. Even in immigration societies such as the United States, this differentiation process is experienced as painful: it is inducing populist reactions everywhere – not exclusively, but especially, among disadvantaged members of societies.

The religious divisions currently being experienced by the populations of European countries as a result of immigration from Islamic countries are an example of an especially heavy burden. On the one hand, the liberal state that guarantees freedom of religion can go a long way towards accommodating the minorities by granting religious and cultural rights. On the other hand, however, it must not make dubious compromises; it must require that minorities practise their cultural way of life and religion only within the framework of basic rights that are equally valid for everyone. In view of the fact that these conflicts can, at best, be alleviated with the legislative and bureaucratic means at the disposal of the state, but can be resolved only through long-term acculturation and socialization, you ask about the mediating role of deliberative politics. It is, of course, helpful when the various integration conflicts are thematized sympathetically in the wider public domain and, above all, when the fears and uncertainties fuelled by populist movements are defused. As you yourself hint at, however, the bare political fact that these problems are becoming topics of public deliberation is almost more important than the arguments themselves; in the first instance, it is how these problems are dealt with that initially opens people's eyes for each other and then may foster mutual respect between self-enclosed groups – the style is the message.

Deliberation as a form of communication is indeed generally closely connected with mutual respect between participants in argumentation. John Rawls understands the mutual respect called for by the public use of reason as a political virtue. This form of respect is directed to the person of another who should be recognized as an equal citizen; in the context of the public use of reason, respect includes the willingness to justify one's political opinion to the other person – that is, to engage in discourse with her. Admittedly, this is only a necessary condition for the *more far-reaching expectation* that, in the course of the discourse, one should also adopt the perspective of one's interlocutor and project oneself into her situation. This sociocognitive achievement is not relevant for discourses about facts, because factual discourses are purely a matter of evaluating arguments. But practical discourses involve disagreements over interests whose relative weights can only be evaluated from the perspective of the lifeworlds of the others involved. This *reciprocal perspective taking*, which is a precondition of adopting the moral point of view on a conflict, does indeed have a purely cognitive function; however, the real obstacle is the *willingness* to engage in this strenuous operation across wide cultural distances in the first place. The need to cross this motivational threshold explains the stubbornness of the conflicts you address – but also, more generally, the fact that empirical and theoretical issues are often easier to resolve consensually than practical conflicts.

If I may conclude with a provocative question: Do you agree that with Between Facts and Norms *you abandoned the terrain of critical theory? That book strongly emphasizes the functioning of the liberal-democratic state, even though this is also a liberal-capitalist state.*

In my theoretical work, I remain committed to the tradition founded by Max Horkheimer and, of course, to my teacher Theodor W. Adorno. The thought of the older generation of critical theorists who were expelled from Germany was dominated by the experiences of fascism and Stalinism. It is only since the Second World War that attempts to tame capitalism through the welfare state have prevailed for the time being, at least in a rather small region of this world. These in retrospect somewhat gilded decades – Eric Hobsbawm spoke half ironically of the 'Golden Age' – have nevertheless shown what the balanced implementation of *both* elements, the rule of law *and* democracy, can achieve, namely, the political *exploitation* of a highly productive economic system to implement the normative content of constitutional democracies. In *Between Facts and Norms* I tried to reconstruct this content. Liberal rights do not fall from the sky. Citizens involved in democratic will formation on a basis of equality first have to be able to understand themselves *as the authors of the rights* that they grant *each other* as members of an association of free and equal individuals. In the light of this recon-struction one can discern all the more clearly the erosion of democracy that has been progressing ever further since politics has more or less abdicated in the face of the systemic pressure of deregulated markets. From this perspective, the theory of democracy and the critique of capitalism belong together. I did not invent the term 'post-democracy'. But the political repercussions of the impacts of the global implementation of neoliberal policies on society can be brought together under it.

What Is Meant by 'Deliberative Democracy'? Objections and Misunderstandings

Modern democracy differs fundamentally from its ancient predecessors in that it represents a political community *constituted* by means of modern law, one which equips its citizens with equal *subjective rights*. Furthermore, it developed in territorial states and is distinguished from the small-scale Greek model above all by its representative character; for, in modern democracies, the citizens can engage in political will formation only indirectly, that is, through *general elections*. The crucial point in our context is that the condition of a *jointly exercised* act of will can only be fulfilled in an inclusive public sphere. For only if the electoral acts are a result of the citizens' participation in *largely anonymous, but jointly conducted, mass communication processes* can these decisions satisfy two requirements: that, as the result of joint will formation, they are made individually and independently by everyone. Public communication is the necessary link connecting the political autonomy of the individual with the joint political will formation of the citizenry as a whole.

This constellation is important, because I am concerned in what follows with a crucial problem that can *only* be solved *through* democratic will formation. For it is only as participants in the process of forming public opinions that individual citizens, when they form opinions and make decisions as individuals, can reconcile the tension between each private citizen's [*Gesellschaftsbürger*] own interests and the interest of public citizens [*Staatsbürger*] in the common good. This tension, which is inherent in the very definition of the democratic constitutional state, must be processed already within the scope of the political decisions of individual citizens, because public citizens must not identify completely with themselves in their role as private citizens, notwithstanding the union of public and private citizen in a single person. The democratic constitutional state guarantees every citizen, *equally originally*, both political autonomy and the equal freedoms of a subject of private law. The legal norms that guarantee such freedoms, Kant's 'coercive laws of freedom', can be willed equally by all only if they reflect a balance between the respective conflicting interests founded on solidarity. And this balance can, in turn, only be achieved in the public sphere by the electorate engaging in joint political processes of opinion and will formation.

Also for present purposes, I would like to begin with some comments on this aspect of modern democracies (1) before explaining why the latter depend on deliberative forms of politics and why the objections raised against this conception – namely, that it is oblivious of power (2) and that its supposed 'orientation to truth' is mistaken (3) – are as groundless as the alternative interpretations proposed by expertocrats and populists (4).

(1) The constitutional state does not fall from the sky. Rather, it is founded by constituent assemblies that are necessarily informed by a *spirit of solidarity*, some element of which *must* also *be perpetuated* in and with this state. In the social contract tradition, this founding act has been imagined in terms of a transition from the state of nature to the state of society. Philosophers at first came up with quite different motives for this transition. Be that as it may, the two constitutional revolutions that actually took place at the end of the eighteenth century were at any rate historical events that owed their existence to the *joint decision* and public negotiations of enterprising citizens. Subsequent generations must not squander the *social capital* of this original founding act. They must make at least modest efforts to constantly *renew* it through continued participation

in the democratic process of political legislation – and sometimes these efforts must even have a counterfactual character (as is the case in Germany, whose Basic Law did not originate in a democratic decision by its citizens).

Even if the *liberal purpose of the constitutional state* is to guarantee equal private liberties to freely associated private citizens in the form of subjective rights, these liberties remain free from paternalistic heteronomy only if *these same* citizens, in their role as public citizens and democratic co-legislators, make use of the rights of communication and participation, which are granted simultaneously, in the spirit of an *intersubjective exercise of political autonomy*. The private liberties of the constitutional state can only correspond to their own interests if citizens confer their rights on themselves. Legislation oriented to the common good must strike a balance between conflicting social interests and seek to compensate for the social inequalities that continually arise in a quasi-natural way in capitalist societies, to such an extent that all citizens receive the same opportunities to lead a *self-determined* life in accordance with their individual conceptions of themselves. All private citizens want a fair opportunity to use their subjective rights to shape their lives. Only in that case will they be motivated and able to make any use of their democratic rights at all, specifically one which is not motivated exclusively by self-interest. In this way, a *self-stabilizing* cycle can become established in which, on the one hand, the autonomous use of civic rights generates, through the legislative process, those subjective rights that (as John Rawls requires) have the same value for all, so that the enjoyment of these rights in turn ensures all citizens the social independence that first enables and enjoins them to make active use of political autonomy. In this way, private and public autonomy must enable and promote each other.

This self-stabilizing cycle, however, has a fault line which shows that different demands are involved in the use citizens should make of their political participation rights and in the use they can make of their private freedoms. The guarantees of both public and private liberty assume the same form, namely, that of subjective rights; but while the legal form of an *entitlement* is tailored to the interest-driven use of the private liberties, it does not fit in the same way with the political obligation to exercise democratic rights. Each citizen is enjoined to make use of her right to vote, and in general her rights of communication and participation, to resolve in a fair and informed manner the problem that the political parties cannot take out of the citizens' hands – namely, that of striking a fair balance between legitimate private interests and public interests in making their political choices. Even if, as a general rule, the democratic state doses this public interest expectation sparingly, every individual, in her role as a public citizen, is involved in solving the problem that every democratic polity inscribes on its banner with its constitutional principles – namely, that all citizens should, by and large, also be able to recognize their own will in the actually implemented laws and freedoms that emerge from the formation of a pluralistic democratic will. No matter how far existing democracies have moved away from this political goal in the meantime – and the oldest among them scandalously ahead of all the rest – they are worthy of being called democracies only as long as the mass of their citizens credibly adhere to this goal.

Because the same subjective rights must also have 'the same value' for each citizen in the long run, they cannot be guaranteed in a politically enduring way without the possibility of *safeguarding coercive law in the political solidarity of the legislating citizens*. This becomes apparent whenever this self-stabilizing circular relationship between legislation with a sufficient public-interest orientation and sufficient satisfaction of the spectrum of private interests falters. In order to contain the swings of a crisis-prone economic system that tends to produce social inequalities, prudent government intervention is needed in any case. Political self-stabilization can fail in a particularly drastic way, however, when wars or disasters place the political community under stress, because it can no longer maintain itself in the customary flexible equilibrium without extraordinary collective efforts.[1] In such cases – or if, as in the case of a pandemic, the challenge is posed by uncontrolled natural processes – the state must muster extraordinary and, if necessary, disproportionately large *forces of solidarity* from its citizens to counter a danger intruding contingently from *the outside* that poses a threat to *the collective as a whole*. In the current exceptional situation created by the COVID-19 pandemic, the state can only exact such *extraordinary* collective efforts at the cost of temporarily regressing below the legal level of mature democracies. Only because such exceptional situations require *a comparatively higher* level of solidarity do the official requirements – in support of the prima facie priority of official protection of public health – *upset* the otherwise customary, *self-stabilizing* circular process between the contributions of citizens to political will formation oriented to the public interest and the intact scope for exercising individual liberties.[2]

In such cases, the extraordinary contributions of solidarity are often no longer recognizable *as such*. In that case, the burdens that must be placed on citizens are still civic contributions to a collective effort that has been democratically decided. But they lose their *voluntary* character because the state must use legal coercion to demand these contributions of solidarity, albeit with legal authorization, for functional reasons alone, even though, legally speaking, they may only be politically expected but not prescribed. If the question of which citizens can be expected to bear which burdens is decided by a will legitimized by the legislature, there can scarcely be any doubt about the legitimacy of mandatory solidarity contributions, because otherwise the state would have to pursue policies that would amount to *accepting* an increase in infection and death rates that is in itself *avoidable*. But such a catastrophe brings to awareness in a drastic way that the inherent structural problem of democratic constitutions of striking a balance between the self-interested exercise of subjective freedoms and the functionally necessary orientation towards the common good must be solved by the citizens themselves – and that this problem can only be solved through a joint process of opinion and will formation in the political public sphere.

In such exceptional situations, it becomes glaringly obvious what is also at stake in the normal case. Contrary to the widespread caricature, democratic politics must not be exhausted by the naked balancing of interests between citizens and organizations making decisions based on private, egoistic motives – it must not be exhausted in unbridled compromises. Rather, it is a matter of striking a balance between the subjective freedoms enjoyed by private citizens as beneficiaries of formally equal rights and the solidarity that public citizens owe one another in their role as co-legislators. For the point of the democratic constitutional state is to ensure that the same individual liberties also have the same de facto value for everyone. The inclusive public communication dominated by mass media is the only place in the democracies of large-scale territorial states in which this process of jointly striking a balance between self-interest and the orientation towards the common good can occur. In the voting booth, only individual opinions are registered; the common element is the context in which these are formed – the cacophony of opinions circulating in the public sphere that condense into competing public opinions.

The theoretical programme of deliberative democracy has gained academic recognition since the early 1990s, initially in the United States.[3] Nevertheless, it repeatedly encounters a number of stereotypical objections, which I would like to address briefly.

(2) The historical association of the notion of deliberative politics with early liberal ideas of 'deliberative assemblies' is sufficient to arouse the suspicion that the notion rests on an idealistic picture of parliamentarism that obscures the hard facts of power-driven realpolitik. Thus, the first objection focuses on the question of why we emphasize the deliberative element in politics,

of all things, although 'politics' primarily means the struggle for power – for acquiring and asserting power and its resources. This objection is implicitly based on the empiricist concept of power that is widespread in sociology. According to this concept, a ruler can rely on the threat potential afforded him by the means of sanction at his disposal to impose his will against the resistance of opponents. But this realist conception of power cannot explain the core element of modern democracies, namely, the fact that majority decisions are accepted on average. With the increasing individualism of the pluralistic societies of the West, unifying worldviews have lost their ability to legitimize power. Without recourse to such metasocial sources of legitimation, democratic constitutional states must draw upon their own resources to legitimize the exercise of ruling functions – namely, by means of the legally institutionalized procedure of democratic (possibly qualified) majority decision-making.

However, the aforementioned sociological concept of power cannot explain how this procedure works. If all that was decided in periodically repeated elections was that the majority is authorized to impose its political will on the minority for a certain period of time, the explanation for the acceptance of the majority principle would be spurious at best. According to the empiricist view of elections, the majority of the votes counted represents an imagined physical superiority of the corresponding majority of the voters themselves; and this supposedly justifies why the political camp of the respective 'predominant' portion of the citizenry 'gets its way', which means a government whose declared goals are based on its preferences rather than on those of the temporarily defeated minority. Since the empiricist notion of power is based on the concept of freedom of choice and action, it sees majority rule as being expressed in the fact that the government guarantees the predominant portion of the population privileged practical scope to pursue its preferences.

Even if the recourse to the threat potential of the superior physical force of a majority of citizens is only supposed to serve as a reserve in case the directives of those in power meet with physical resistance, this version would scarcely provide an adequate explanation of the underpinnings of a political order based on human rights. A self-determining association of free and equal legal subjects is founded on the idea of the self-empowerment of each citizen only to obey those laws that she has given herself based on a political process of opinion and will formation in which she engages with all other citizens. This demanding idea cannot be redeemed using the empiricist notions of power and freedom according to which majority decisions are legitimized by aggregating the numbers of 'raw' preferences of all participants. Instead, democratic elections must be understood *as the final stage of a problem-solving process*, that is, as the result of a joint formation of opinion and will by citizens who first *form their preferences* in the course of a public, more or less rational debate over how to deal with the problems requiring political regulation.

This element of deliberation as preparation for making decisions is an essential part of the explanation of how the democratic procedure also legitimizes majority decisions in the eyes of the defeated minority. From the participant perspective, the persuasiveness of the procedure is explained by an unlikely combination of two features: on the one hand, this requires the participation of all persons who may be affected by the outcome; on the other hand, it makes the decision itself dependent on the more or less discursive character of the preceding deliberation. The condition of inclusiveness corresponds to the democratic requirement that *all* those potentially affected should *participate*, while the filter of the deliberative exchange of proposals, information and reasons justifies the *assumption* that the result is *rationally acceptable*. This assumption can be tested in turn against the deliberative quality of the preceding deliberations. Such discourses are expected to mobilize competition between relevant public opinions based on germane topics, requisite information and pertinent pro and contra stances. In short, the coupling of inclusive participation with discursive deliberation explains *the expectation that the results are rationally acceptable*. Because every decision means that a discourse is being broken off, however, the defeated minorities can also accept majority decisions without having to abandon their own convictions in the hope that their arguments will be successful in the long run.

(3) Another objection is directed against the assumption that political debates are oriented towards 'truth' at all, and thus towards the goal of reaching agreement. Don't political discourses have a manifestly polemical character and hence seem to demand a description that captures their intrinsically agonal nature? But it is precisely the 'orientation towards truth' – that is, the conviction or feeling of those involved that their opinions and assessments are 'right' – that fuels political controversies and lends them their contentious character. Admittedly, we need to differentiate here, because while many things are disputed in politics, only assertoric statements can be true or false in the strict sense. Of course, the claims to validity we associate – going beyond factual statements – with moral or juridical statements about justice, for example, can also be correct or mistaken; they can be treated *like* claims to truth in discourses. And even statements that are not associated with binary-coded validity claims can be defended or criticized on more or less

convincing grounds. Even ethical-political statements that, from the point of view of a political community or a subculture, are a matter of the preferability of certain values over secondary values or, in general, of identification with certain forms of life, can be rendered plausible using reasons. Unlike expressions of preferences, ethical and even aesthetic expressions also assert claims to validity in the space of reasons. Preferences, like desires, only admit of subjective expression or, as subjective *claims*, they can only be justified in the light of valid norms. In short, if one grasps the logical form of practical questions and remembers that politics essentially touches on those questions which are negotiated, beyond self-referential interests, from moral, legal and ethical-political points of view, it also becomes clear that public political disputes, even when they go beyond contentious factual questions, are conducted in the discursive space of the exchange of reasons. This is also true of compromises, i.e. of most of the controversial political issues, because compromises operate within a legal framework and are subject in turn to considerations of fairness.

The reference to the agonal trait of politics only yields an objection to the conception of deliberative politics if we confuse the *intention of the participants* – who, with their utterances, want to make an epistemic (i.e. a justified and rationally criticizable) contribution to the debate – with the naïve *expectation* that agreement could be reached here and now in political discussions; for the pressure to make decisions means that political discussions, unlike the 'infinite conversation' of philosophers, are always subject to time limits. It is precisely the awareness of the pressure to decide that lends the attitude in which arguments based on practical reason are presented and defended its impatient character and sharpness of tone. At the same time, all parties involved are aware that at best reasonable, but for the time being only *competing*, public opinions can – and should – be generated in the mass communication of the public sphere steered by the media. The citizens should be able to make informed decisions, each for him- or herself, in the voting booth in the light of these public opinions. It is only in parliaments and other state institutions that legally binding decisions can be made face to face following democratic *deliberation*. However, the election results must be processed at the further levels of the political system so that voters gain the impression over the course of the legislative period that the output, i.e. the policies actually implemented, stands in a recognizable relation to the voters' input and their orientation to the election promises of the party or parties charged with governing.

In order to legitimize the government, the political system must do more than merely produce satisfactory results. For unless the democratic vote is connected in *recognizable* ways with what voters actually 'receive', political rule becomes an autonomous paternalistic regime. In other words, once the function of the political public sphere decays, the state loses its democratic substance, even if the 'rule of law' remains unaffected and the government more or less satisfies its voters. This latent danger can only be averted in the large-scale polities of the modern era insofar as the media infrastructure of the public sphere enables halfway deliberative opinion and will formation by the population itself. The independent media must generate sufficient power of articulation to maintain the connection of political power back to the communicative power generated by the citizens, the only 'power' that 'proceeds' from the people.

On the other hand, democratically legitimized rule also requires a government that has confidence in its political power to make policy. Merely giving the *appearance* of a democratically steered leadership is not enough. The *opinion poll-driven* politics characteristic of the currently dominant political style of maintaining power by opportunistically adapting policy to systemic constraints is undemocratic, because it both calls into question the state's capacity for political action and circumvents political opinion and will formation in civil society and in the political public sphere. When the political elites become paralysed by the defeatism nurtured by systems theory, the population cannot fail to lose faith in governments that only pretend to be able and willing to act.

(4) Correcting misunderstandings that plague the concept of deliberative politics directs our attention to empirically quite demanding normative presuppositions of the democratic constitutional state and thus provokes the objection that the proposed reading is excessively idealistic. Therefore, there are good reasons to consider two of the currently prevailing alternative readings, in order to examine whether – while acknowledging the concern to deflate high-flown normative claims – they can be reconciled with at least the core content of democratic constitutions.[4] One side takes the pluralistic surface phenomena of the 'raw', so to speak, spontaneous and authentic will of the electorate as its starting point, while the other side, conversely, represents the expert judgement of the political elite as relatively independent of the verdict of the electorate and public opinion. Both alternatives ignore in equal measure the relevance of an enlightened and inclusive formation of opinion and will by the citizens in the political public sphere. Thus relieved of a normatively demanding expectation, these readings can boast that they are 'realistic' in a certain sense; but then the

political regression we are currently witnessing raises the pressing question as to what happens to democracies in which the political public sphere disintegrates and the interplay between political parties and public opinion wanes.

For the 'pluralist' approach, the claim of a democratic constitution is sufficiently fulfilled with the procedure of 'free elections', because the statistical aggregation of votes ensures that each citizen's vote is counted equally, hence fairly, and in this formal sense comes 'into play'. This minimalist reading ignores the question of how the democratic vote comes about. In general elections, however, the summation and distribution of individual votes determines which among the competing forces should govern the country and with which declared objectives. The result, therefore, regardless of the fact that it is composed of many autonomously cast individual votes, concerns all of the citizens in common; it is 'their' government to which the voters have bound themselves with their vote. Since each individual already expects such an institutional result – i.e. one that has far-reaching consequences for all citizens alike – when she casts her vote, it would only be consistent if the individual election decisions had proceeded from a corresponding, i.e. *joint*, political decision-making process. Therefore, the alleged advantage of the pluralistic approach, which regards the mode of opinion and will formation from an individualistic point of view as a private matter of the individual, obscures an essential aspect. Specifically, it ignores the actual task of democratic citizens, which is to integrate the individual interests that each of them has as a private citizen with what is in the shared interest of all citizens.

The 'expertocratic' approach is also realistic insofar as it highlights the slim budget of time, motivation, attention and cognitive effort that ordinary citizens, preoccupied with their professional and personal lives, expend on their role as citizens. At the same time, it reminds us of the growing complexity of the tasks that government and administration have to cope with in modern societies. The complexity of the various self-regulating societal subsystems does tend to relieve the pressure on a state organization that has itself become an independent functional system. But when the political experts become the default option for repairing the malfunctions of almost all other functional subsystems, or even when they pursue constructive political goals, they have to acquire diverse and detailed expertise. Therefore, the argument goes, politics inevitably overtaxes not only the citizen's willingness to respond and their attention, but also their ability to respond. The allegedly unbridgeable gulf between the specialized knowledge required to deal with the problems and common sense makes it impossible, according to the technocratic view, to involve the citizens themselves seriously in the formation of opinions about political alternatives. Moreover, this seems to be confirmed by the plebiscitary character of the election campaigns: party manifestos that no one reads are replaced by professional advertising for candidates. This description is also not unrealistic. But the price the citizens pay for this deficit is, in turn, the renunciation of any meaningful use of their political autonomy.

The 'realism' of the two approaches is a result of the fact that they stylize empirically well-documented traits of will formation in Western mass democracies. At the same time, they suggest that these traits, whether or not they are regarded as normative deficits, are *inevitable* under modern social conditions. But the evidence for this more far-reaching statement is far from convincing. The growing pluralism of our societies is a matter of the multiplication of cultural forms of life and individual lifestyles; as a result, there is a general trend in large-scale societies for the burden of social integration to shift from the level of socialized lifeworlds to that of political citizenship, whereby integration via citizenship becomes detached from national, i.e. pre-political, ties. But if social cohesion must increasingly be secured at the more abstract level of citizenship, this functional imperative speaks all the more strongly in favour of mobilizing political opinion and will formation; the digital infrastructure would also be more or less favourable to such a development, but only on the condition that it is subjected to a corresponding regulation, which for the time being is lacking. Something similar holds true for the disparity between the expertise of the political experts and the *capacity to respond* of the civic common sense of the citizens. It is true that the work of governments and administrations also requires a high level of expertise. But aside from the fact that politicians are themselves in need of advice from their experts, it is simply not true that complex political considerations cannot be translated into everyday language that interested citizens (i.e. all of us) can understand – otherwise they would not be *political* considerations. Especially in view of the general directions of political programmes and when it comes to weighing up corresponding alternatives, it is a question of clever and skilful professional translation whether the essence of the matter and its justification is captured by an explanation expressed in normal language. And the scepticism concerning citizens' *willingness to participate in politics* under normal circumstances would have to be re-examined in view of the surprising level of political commitment that we are currently witnessing in the wake of growing right-wing radicalism. This does not confirm scepticism concerning the ability and willingness to respond to political messages even among strata that tend to be of lower social status and have a comparatively lower level of formal education. In populations that are becoming increasingly intelligent, as measured by levels of general schooling, a corresponding education for political participation need not fail per se because it is outweighed by citizens' private interests.

Precisely the disturbing combination of traditional right-wing populism – 'We are the people' – with the libertarian self-centredness of freaked-out conspiracy theorists, who defend their individual liberties against imagined oppression by an allegedly merely sham democratic constitutional state, is reason enough to turn the tables. In the on the whole growing capitalist societies of our – as it now transpires – not particularly stable democracies, this surprising potential for resistance develops and causes the political system to crumble from within once growing social inequalities have sufficiently undermined the political public sphere.

Notes

Preface

1 Martin Seeliger and Sebastian Sevignani (eds.), *Ein erneuter Strukturwandel der Öffentlichkeit?* (*Leviathan*, Special Issue 37) (Baden-Baden: Nomos, 2021). For English translations of selected contributions, see Seeliger and Sevignani (eds.), 'Special Issue: A New Structural Transformation of the Public Sphere?', *Theory, Culture & Society* 39/4 (2022).

2 Jürgen Habermas, 'Interview', in André Bächtiger, John S. Dryzek, Jane Mansbridge and Mark E. Warren (eds.), *The Oxford Handbook of Deliberative Democracy* (Oxford: Oxford University Press, 2018), pp. 871–82.

3 Jürgen Habermas, 'Foreword', in Emilie Prattico (ed.), *Habermas and the Crisis of Democracy: Interviews with Leading Thinkers* (London and New York: Routledge, 2022), xiii–xix.

Reflections and Conjectures on a New Structural Transformation of the Public Sphere

1   An earlier version of this chapter was published as Jürgen Habermas, 'Reflections and Hypotheses on a Further Structural Transformation of the Political Public Sphere', *Theory, Culture & Society* 39/4 (2022): 145–71.

2   Martin Seeliger and Sebastian Sevignani (eds.), *Ein erneuter Strukturwandel der Öffentlichkeit?* (*Leviathan*, Special Issue 37) (Baden-Baden: Nomos, 2021). See Habermas, *The Structural Transformation of the Public Sphere: An Inquiry into a Category of Bourgeois Society*, trans. Thomas Burger and Frederick Lawrence (Cambridge: Polity, 1989); originally published as: *Strukturwandel der Öffentlichkeit: Untersuchungen zu einer Kategorie der bürgerlichen Gesellschaft* (Neuwied: Luchterhand and Frankfurt am Main: Suhrkamp, 1962).

3   Bernhard Peters, *Die Integration moderner Gesellschaften* (Frankfurt am Main: Suhrkamp, 1993), and Peters, 'On Public Deliberation and Public Culture: Reflections on the Public Sphere', in Hartmut Wessler (ed.), *Public Deliberation and Public Culture: The Writings of Bernhard Peters, 1993–2005* (London: Palgrave Macmillan), pp. 134–59; from this perspective, see also Hartmut Wessler, *Habermas and the Media* (Cambridge: Polity, 2018).

4   On the relationship between the political and literary public spheres, see my sidelong glance in Habermas, 'Warum nicht lesen?', in Katharina Raabe and Frank Wagner (eds.), *Warum Lesen – mindestens 24 Gründe* (Berlin: Suhrkamp, 2020), pp. 99–123.

5 The chapter on the role of civil society and the political public sphere in *Between Facts and Norms* – Habermas, *Between Facts and Norms: Contributions to a Discourse Theory of Law and Democracy*, trans. William Rehg (Cambridge, MA: MIT Press, 1996), pp. 329–87 – takes up the reflections in the concluding chapter of *Structural Transformation of the Public Sphere*, and especially in the introduction to the new 1990 edition of *Strukturwandel der Öffentlichkeit*: Habermas, 'Further Reflections on the Public Sphere', in Craig Calhoun (ed.), *Habermas and the Public Sphere* (Cambridge, MA: MIT Press, 1992), pp. 421–61. For more recent reflections on the topic, see Habermas, 'Political Communication in Media Society: Does Democracy Still Have an Epistemic Dimension? The Impact of Normative Theory on Empirical Research', in *Europe: The Faltering Project*, trans. Ciaran Cronin (Cambridge: Polity, 2009), pp. 138–83.

6 Usually, however, sociological theories choose a basic conceptual approach that leaves the cognitive meaning of this dimension of validity out of account and attributes the binding effect of ought-validity [*Sollgeltung*] to the threat of sanctions.

7 The text of the French Constitution of September 1791 opens with a catalogue that distinguishes between *droits naturels* and *droits civils*. In this way, it took into account the temporal discrepancy between the current domain of validity of the general civil rights and the as yet unrealized claim to validity, which extends far beyond the territorial boundaries of the French state, of the 'natural' rights to

which all persons have an equal claim in virtue of their humanity. Paradoxically, however, the human and civil rights enshrined as basic rights preserve the meaning of universal rights within national borders as well. In this way, they remind the present and future generations, if not of a self-obligation to actively propagate these rights, then at least of the peculiar character of the *context-transcending normative* content of universal human rights beyond the provisionality of their *at present* territorially restricted implementation. The moral surplus also leaves traces of an as yet unexhausted normative content in the existing basic rights, which exhibit something of the troubling character of an *unsaturated* norm. The lack of 'saturation' concerns the *temporal* dimension of the *exhaustion* – which, in the political community, is still pending and whose content still needs to be specified – of the indeterminate, context-transcending substance of established basic rights, as well as the *spatial* dimension of a *worldwide* implementation of human rights that remains to be accomplished.

8   See Daniel Gaus, 'Rational Reconstruction as a Method of Political Theory between Social Critique and Empirical Political Science', *Constellations* 20/4 (2013): 553–70.

9   See 'Interview with Jürgen Habermas', in André Bächtiger et al. (eds.), *The Oxford Handbook of Deliberative Democracy*, pp. 871–82.

10 On this, see Habermas, 'Political Communication in Media Society'. See also Habermas, 'On the Internal

Relation between the Rule of Law and Democracy', *European Journal of Philosophy* 3/1 (1995): 12–20.

11 *Vormärz* (lit. 'pre-March') refers to the period of revolutionary uprisings across the German states, and Europe in general, prior to March 1848, when a constituent assembly was convened in the Paulskirche in Frankfurt. The resulting attempt to establish a liberal democratic national constitution in the German states foundered in the following year on monarchist resistance and dwindling popular support. [*Trans.*]

12 Martin Seeliger and Sebastian Sevignani specify this role in terms of the transparency of public issues, the general orientation of citizens and the reciprocal justification of topics and contributions. See Seeliger and Sevignani, 'A New Structural Transformation of the Public Sphere? An Introduction', *Theory, Culture & Society* 39/4 (2022): 3–16, here p. 11.

13 Normatively speaking, the so-called output legitimacy of government action that keeps citizens happy does not meet the conditions of democratically legitimate action; for although such services of the state coincide with citizens' interests, they do not satisfy their interests *by executing a democratically formed will* of the citizens themselves.

14 See my review of Cristina Lafont: Habermas, 'Commentary on Cristina Lafont, *Democracy Without Shortcuts*', *Journal of Deliberative Democracy* 16/2 (2020): 10–14.

15 Article 20 para. 2 of the Basic Law, the German federal

constitution, declares that 'All state authority is derived from the people.' [*Trans.*]

16 See Rainer Forst, *Toleration in Conflict: Past and Present*, trans. Ciaran Cronin (Cambridge: Cambridge University Press, 2013).

17 On the political concept of solidarity, see Habermas, *The Lure of Technocracy*, trans. Ciaran Cronin (Cambridge: Polity, 2015), pp. 98–100.

18 See Armin Schäfer, *Der Verlust politischer Gleichheit* (Frankfurt am Main: Campus, 2015).

19 See Armin Schäfer and Michael Zürn, *Die demokratische Regression* (Berlin: Suhrkamp, 2021).

20 The phenomenon of contemporary right-wing populism illustrates how, in reasonably stable democracies, the steep *normative gradient* between the idea of deliberative politics, on the one hand, and the sobering reality of opinion and will formation, on the other, is anchored in social reality itself *through the intuitions of the citizens*. Empirical studies on voting behaviour, the level of information and political awareness of the population, political parties' professional election advertising, public relations, campaign strategies, etc., have long since enabled us to form a realistic picture of political opinion and will formation; but neither these facts themselves nor knowledge of them normally shake the assumption of the active and passive electorate that the 'will of the voters', whether one agrees with the outcome or not, is sufficiently respected and sets the agenda for future policies. As the derogatory references to the established

political parties in current German political discourse as 'system parties' shows, however, even such *forbearing* normative assumptions can become inverted into their opposite once confidence in them among the population at large is enduringly shaken. Then 'we' are the people which knows what is true and what is false, while a bridge cannot be constructed to the 'others' even with arguments.

21 In contemporary German public discourse, 'the disconnected' [*die Abgehängten*] refers to groups of citizens who for various reasons feel disconnected from the political process or abandoned by the mainstream political parties and, in recent years, have tended to identify with or actively support mainly right-wing opposition movements (such as those that rallied against the public measures to combat the COVID-19 pandemic) and political parties (in particular, the Alternative for Germany). [*Trans.*]

22 See Philipp Staab and Thorsten Thiel, 'Social Media and the Digital Structural Transformation of the Public Sphere', *Theory, Culture & Society* 39/4 (2022): 129–43.

23 See Habermas, *The Crisis of the European Union*, trans. Ciaran Cronin (Cambridge: Polity, 2012).

24 See Michael Zürn, 'Öffentlichkeit und Global Governance', in Seeliger and Sevignani (eds.), *Ein erneuter Strukturwandel der Öffentlichkeit?*, pp. 160–87.

25 Jürg Steiner, André Bächtiger, Markus Spörndli and Marco R. Steenbergen, *Deliberative Politics in Action* (Cambridge: Cambridge University Press, 2004).

26 The global expansion of accelerated and multiplied

communication flows leads Claudia Ritzi to suggest that, rather than the image of the centre and periphery, 'the concept of the "universe" is a better metaphor for describing contemporary political publics. It creates an awareness of the unboundedness of the contemporary public space.' See Ritzi, 'Libration im Öffentlichkeitsuniversum', in Seeliger and Sevignani (eds.), *Ein erneuter Strukturwandel der Öffentlichkeit?*, pp. 298–319, here p. 305.

27 See Sebastian Sevignani, 'Digital Transformations and the Ideological Formation of the Public Sphere: Hegemonic, Populist, or Popular Communication?', *Theory, Culture & Society* 39/4 (2022): 91–109.

28 In what follows, I am relying on my correspondence with – and on the interpretive proposals of – Jürgen Gerhards, who drew my attention to the results of the ARD/ZDF long-term study on mass communication between 1964 and 2020. The autumn 2019 Eurobarometer also provides data that permit further conclusions.

29 See Shoshana Zuboff, *The Age of Surveillance Capitalism: The Fight for a Human Future at the New Frontier of Power* (New York: Public Affairs, 2018).

30 See Christian Fuchs, 'Soziale Medien und Öffentlichkeit', in Fuchs, *Das digitale Kapital: Zur Kritik der politischen Ökonomie des 21. Jahrhunderts* (Vienna: Mandelbaum, 2021), 235–72.

31 Otfried Jarren and Renate Fischer, 'Die Plattformisierung von Öffentlichkeit und der Relevanzverlust des Journalismus als demokratische Herausforderung', in

Seeliger and Sevignani (eds.), *Ein erneuter Strukturwandel der Öffentlichkeit?*, pp. 365–84.

32 Ibid., p. 370.

33 See Staab and Thiel, 'Social Media and the Digital Structural Transformation of the Public Sphere'; Andreas Reckwitz, *The Society of Singularities*, trans. Valentine A. Pakis (Cambridge: Polity, 2020).

34 A consistent exception to this is, of course, literary correspondence, which – as the pertinent example of the Romantics demonstrates – satisfies aesthetic standards and thus also a public interest.

35 Regrettably, here I cannot address the more far-reaching reflections of Hans-Jörg Trenz, 'Öffentlichkeitstheorie als Erkenntnistheorie moderner Gesellschaft', in Seeliger and Sevignani (eds.), *Ein erneuter Strukturwandel der Öffentlichkeit?*, pp. 385–405.

36 See W. Lance Bennett and Barbara Pfetsch, 'Rethinking Political Communication in a Time of Disrupted Public Spheres', *Journal of Communication* 68/2 (2018): 243–53.

37 See also the vivid presentation in Andreas Barthelmes, *Die große Zerstörung: Was der digitale Bruch mit unserem Leben macht* (Berlin: Duden, 2020), esp. Ch. 7, pp. 128–55.

38 This 'semi-public sphere' can be described equally well as a semi-privatized public sphere; Philipp Staab and Thorsten Thiel capture this character when they speak of 'privatisation without privatism'. See Staab and Thiel, 'Social Media and the Digital Structural Transformation of the Public Sphere', p. 140.

39 Romy Jaster and David Lanius, 'Fake News in Politik und Öffentlichkeit', in Ralf Hohlfeld, Michael Harnischmacher, Elfi Heinke, Lea Lehner and Michael Sengl (eds.), *Fake News und Desinformation* (Baden-Baden: Nomos, 2020), pp. 245–69.

40 On Trump and fake news, see Michael Oswald, 'Der Begriff "Fake News" als rhetorisches Mittel des Framings in der politischen Kommunikation', in Hohlfeld et al. (eds.), *Fake News und Desinformation*, pp. 61–82.

41 See Ralf Hohlfeld, 'Die Post-Truth-Ära: Kommunikation im Zeitalter von gefühlten Wahrheiten und Alternativen Fakten', in Hohlfeld et al. (eds.), *Fake News und Desinformation*, pp. 43–60.

42 For a plausible statement of the position, see Sebastian Berg, Niklas Rakowski and Thorsten Thiel, *The Digital Constellation* (Weizenbaum Series, 14) (Berlin: Weizenbaum Institute for the Networked Society – The German Internet Institute, 2020); available at: https://doi.org/10.34669/wi.ws/14 (last accessed 15.03.2023).

43 Anyone who understands this connection will recognize the ultimately authoritarian character, directed against the foundations of a discursive public sphere, of the contemporary rampant criticism of the facilities and programme scope of the public broadcasters. Together with the quality press, which will probably soon also require public support to ensure its economic viability, the television and radio broadcasters are for the time being resisting the pull of a 'platformization' of the public sphere and a commodification of public

consciousness. On this, see Fuchs, 'Soziale Medien und Öffentlichkeit'.

Deliberative Democracy: An Interview

1 Jürgen Habermas, "Wahrheitstheorien," in *Vorstudien und Ergänzungen zur Theorie des kommunikativen Handelns* (Frankfurt am Main: Suhrkamp, 1984), pp. 127–86.

2 Daniel Gaus, 'Discourse Theory's Sociological Claim: Reconstructing the Epistemic Meaning of Democracy as a Deliberative System', *Philosophy and Social Criticism* 42/6 (2015): 503–25.

3 Mark E. Warren and Jane Mansbridge, with André Bächtiger et al., 'Deliberative Negotiation', in Mansbridge and Cathie Jo Martin (eds.), *Political Negotiation: A Handbook* (Washington, DC: Brookings Institution Press, 2016), pp. 141–97.

What Is Meant by 'Deliberative Democracy'? Objections and Misunderstandings

1 On the following section, see Habermas, 'Corona und der Schutz des Lebens: Zur Grundrechtsdebatte in der pandemischen Ausnahmesituation', *Blätter für deutsche und internationale Politik* 9 (2021): 65–78.

2 Of course, this is not only true of catastrophes, i.e. contingent dangers intruding from outside, but also in a *different way* of social conflicts, when social strata or cultural groups that feel neglected, that are oppressed or even just insecure split off from the rest of the population and 'drop out' of the shared political culture as opposition

against the system. In some places, the two potentials seem to be combined in the mixture of COVID-19 deniers and right-wing extremists.

3 James Bohman and William Rehg (eds.), *Deliberative Democracy: Essays on Reason and Politics* (Cambridge, MA: MIT Press, 1997); recently: Cristina Lafont, *Democracy without Shortcuts: A Participatory Conception of Deliberative Democracy* (Oxford: Oxford University Press, 2020).

4 On this criticism, see most recently Lafont, *Democracy without Shortcuts*.